D0897697

BOBBY CLARKE AND THE FEROCIOUS FLYERS

Bobby Clarke and the Ferocious Flyers

by STAN FISCHLER

Illustrated with photographs

DODD, MEAD & COMPANY

NEW YORK

ISBN: 0-396-06885-5
Library of Congress Catalog Card Number: 73-15031

Printed in the United States of America
by The Cornwall Press, Inc., Cornwall, N. Y.

To Larry Zeidel, who first planted the seed for my sprouting affection for the Flyers.

Acknowledgements

The author wishes to thank the following for their valuable assistance in preparing this manuscript: Larry Zeidel, Frank Bertucci, Al Robbins, Richard Friedman, Andrew Kulak, Howard Hyman, Joe Kadlec, and, of course, my favorite editor.

Contents

III   The Ferocious Flyers

I

The Magnificent Bobby Clarke

1/

Growing Up in Flin Flon

Among the faraway places with strange sounding names, few equal Flin Flon, Manitoba, the birthplace of Robert Earle "Bobby" Clarke, center and captain of the Philadelphia Flyers.

The name itself is a curio. Because Flin Flon is actually a shortened version of Josiah Flintabbatey Flonatin, hero of a 1905 English dime novel. J. F. Flonatin explored the depths of a bottomless lake in a submarine, and later discovered a city of gold. And there his story ended.

That, in itself, would not have been enough to coin a name for the little city in Northern Manitoba. Flin Flon remained basically undiscovered—and still unnamed—past the turn of the 20th century until 1913 when five prospectors, led by Tom Creighton, headed north from the metropolis of Winnipeg to search for riches.

Along the route Creighton found a tattered book. Picking it up, he discovered the book was eminently readable. Authored by one J. E. Preston-Muddock, it was called *The Sunless City* and had as its hero Professor Josiah Flintabbatey

Flonatin. Creighton was intrigued with Professor Flonatin's exploits and remembered them two years later when he was crossing a lake, went through the ice, built a fire in a cave to dry out, and noticed rich ore under the melted snow.

The episode reminded Creighton of the hole "old Flin Flon" escaped from. So not long afterward, when the men staked the site, it was only natural that they named their claim Flin Flon.

Like Josiah Flintabbatey Flonatin, Tom Creighton and his pals discovered a city of gold; only this one was real. On the site they also found deposits of copper, zinc, and silver. They were in business for life—or for as long as they wanted to remain in Flin Flon.

In 1927 the boys were bought out by the Hudson Bay Mining and Smelting Company. At the time, Hudson Bay Mining and Smelting was principally owned by the American millionaire Cornelius Vanderbilt.

Although the area around Flin Flon is rock—there isn't a cow or chicken or pig on the land anywhere—and everything must be imported from the south, the town on the great rock ridge prospered through the Twenties and, by 1932, had developed enough pride to establish a museum of its own.

Officials at Hudson Bay Mining and Smelting—known affectionately as "The Company"—decided that the first exhibit should be a copy of the book about Professor Flonatin. The mine offered a reward of $500 for such a copy and placed newspaper advertisements in Europe and the United States. Three years later a bookseller in Sussex, England, produced one copy and sent it to Flin Flon with a bill for 70 cents!

Flin Flon continued growing into a sub-Arctic metropolis

of 10,000, mostly because of the mine which goes down 5000 feet and has 50 miles or more of underground tracking on 70 different levels. Curiously, the mine straddles the Saskatchewan–Manitoba border, making for some interesting happenings below ground.

"Since the border runs smack through the middle of the plant," said Canadian author Paul King, "if a miner gets hurt underground, he makes sure it's in the right province—for better compensation."

Like so many frontier mining towns, Flin Flon has developed a series of legends; some true, others as fictional as *The Sunless City*. "They tell one," Paul King recalls, "about how an old prospector got a bunch of chippies in his hotel room, and when they asked him how to use snowshoes, he ordered hundreds of boxes of *Corn Flakes*, dumped them along the corridor, and showed them."

Another story tells about a collection of miners who came off an early morning shift, sought shelter from the sub-zero weather in an empty tarpaper shack, and found an awful lot of liquor. Neither the liquor nor the firewood sufficiently warmed them so they tore down the walls of the cabin for *more* firewood. The next day the bootlegger tenant returned to find he had lost four walls and a roof but gained six sleeping drunks.

Obviously, Flin Flon has been the butt of Canadian jokesmiths, from Vancouver to Halifax. After all, it is 500 miles *north* of Winnipeg, which is pretty far north already, and it is, basically, just a pile of rock. The golf course was cut from stone. The houses are all built on rock—without basements—and some of the streets still have board sidewalks.

"It's a great town," says Tom Dobson, publisher of *The*

Flin Flon Daily Reminder. "We've got every nationality here except Japanese, but there's no separate social standards. We're all wrapped up in one, big, happy family. And the kids are so involved with sports, I don't think we've ever produced a criminal here."

Such was the environment into which Bobby Clarke was born on August 13, 1949. He was the first, and only, son of Cliff and Yvonne Clarke (they later had a daughter, Roxanne) and he began to play hockey immediately upon abandoning his high-chair, give or take a year.

The Clarkes were at 59 Hill Street then but when Bobby was four years old, they moved to 120 Riverside Drive, where the family still lives. "Bobby learned to skate at Lakeside Park," his mother remembers. "It was an open-air rink and he lived there, morning, noon, and night. As long as there was ice, he'd be out there practicing.

"Of course, that still wasn't enough hockey for him so we had another rink out in the garden. Many's the time he'd shoot the puck off the side of our house—and a few times through the windows."

When Bobby was still very young, his father took him on a trip to Winnipeg, the metropolis of Manitoba and the Canadian prairies.

"I figured he'd get a kick going down to Winnipeg," said Cliff, "and seeing all those bright lights. But when we got there he walked down the street, found an outdoor rink with a kids' hockey game, and spent the night watching them bat the puck around. That was Bobby's idea of a good time in the big city!"

Cliff Clarke never formally coached a hockey team but he

was always around to help his eager son and, occasionally, father and son would play in the men-against-the-boys contests.

The first-hand, pulsating thrill of organized hockey didn't penetrate Bobby until 1957 when Flin Flon's best club, the Junior Bombers, defeated Sam Pollock's Hull-Ottawa Canadiens to win the Memorial Cup, emblematic of Canada's junior championship. "The Canadiens," wrote Toronto columnist Paul Rimstead, "went hippity-hopping up to Flin Flon and got walloped."

It was clear that Dream One on Bobby Clarke's agenda was climbing the local hockey ladder to the Bombers. His first coach, Earl Garinger, had doubts about the kid's potential. Bobby was on the skinny side and wasn't a particularly good skater.

"He was a strange skater," Garinger recalls. "Most kids who start out have trouble with their ankles bending in, but only one of Bobby's ankles bent *out*! This worried his dad a great deal. I told Cliff not to worry about it; that the ankle would straighten itself out in time. And it did."

Garinger taught Bobby at three different phases in his early hockey education: at the very beginning; when he was eight years old; and, again, when young Clarke was 11. "At first," said Garinger, "he'd come to the rink in the back of my house. That's where he first learned to stickhandle because we'd have a solid mass of boys—on a 30 by 40 foot rink—not to mention a few girls who came on the ice to do some figure skating.

"Bobby was a quiet boy at the time; somewhat on the shy side. When he was eight he played on our team, the West-

7

leys, and he had one outstanding quality: he was involved. Whatever I said interested him. He was a nice kid; not rambunctious like some of the others.

"Three years later I had him again but he hadn't changed much. He was a more or less average hockey player then. You would certainly never have guessed he'd be a future star."

By now Bobby had grown enough to play in the Flin Flon Arena, a 2000-seat rink that, by contemporary standards, is frontier-style. "You sit watching a hockey game in the Flin Flon Arena," Paul Rimstead observes, "and you say to yourself, this is what hockey is all about. This is hockey before sophistication; before people started talking about this newfangled thing called education. This is hockey as it used to be."

Playing for the Bombers in those days would unspoil any athlete. Flin Flon's nearest opponent was 500 miles away, in Winnipeg. Which meant a 10-hour bus ride—night and day —and very tired young men.

"The people in Flin Flon should join a European league," kids former pro Eddie Dorohoy, "and play against Russia. Heck, they're only a day away."

The prospects of endless, boring bus rides never bothered Bobby and when he reached his early teens his hockey ability took a sudden sharp turn for the better. In the autumn of 1966 he came out for the Bombers and made the team. The Clarkes were delighted, but somewhat concerned.

"We were a little worried about his diabetes," says Mrs. Clarke. "But it turned out that we were a lot more concerned than Bobby was. Then we thought about it and realized that he was so healthy; had never been sick; took

8

good care of himself and never missed any games because of it; so his hockey-playing was okay with us." And it was okay with Pat Ginnell, coach of the Bombers.

Ginnell wasn't sure that Bobby was a champion the first time he saw him, but he didn't send the kid home either. "He was wearing glasses," recalls Ginnell, "and looked kind of thin when he got on the ice. But once he started moving, there was no doubt in my mind that this was going to be one of the best kids I ever coached."

2/
Diabetic—and a Winner

It was difficult to determine whether Pat Ginnell, coach of the Flin Flon Bombers, did more worrying about his center Bobby Clarke, or more applauding his young virtuoso as the kid matured from an obscure, skinny face in the crowd to a teenage superstar.

"He never played a bad game for me," says Ginnell. "Never. Once Bobby started to fill out there was no stopping him."

During the 1967–68 season Bobby scored 51 goals in 59 games for the Flin Flon Bombers, as well as 117 assists for a league-leading 168 points. Based on arithmetic alone, there was no question that he would be one of the highest selections in the National Hockey League junior draft when Clarke graduated from amateur hockey at the end of the 1968–69 season. But . . .

Unfortunately for Bobby's reputation, word had filtered up and down the NHL scouting grapevine that he was a diabetic and certainly could not be counted upon to absorb the rigors of big-league hockey without suffering serious side effects. "Forget about Bobby Clarke!" they whispered often enough for Ginnell to finally hear and take positive action.

"I knew that Bobby wanted to be a professional hockey player," notes Ginnell, "and I knew he'd never get there as long as he had the diabetes rap against him. I figured that there was only one thing to do and that was to have the best doctors determine just how bad, or good, his health really was and what kind of future he might have as a big-league player."

Ginnell arranged for Clarke to visit the famed Mayo Clinic in Rochester, Minnesota. His coach personally escorted him there before the 1968–69 season. Following a battery of tests, the doctors agreed that there was absolutely no reason why Bobby could not play professional hockey *provided he took good care of himself*. What's more, the doctors put it in writing.

"That was all I needed," Ginnell said. "We went home and when the scouts came around the following season I showed them the letter. I wanted everyone from any NHL team who came to Flin Flon to know about Bobby exactly what the doctors at Mayo Clinic knew."

On the ice, Clarke looked like the healthiest 19-year-old in Canada during the 1968–69 season. A neutral observer might question his decision to quit school at 17, but Flin Flon is a world of its own.

"What is entirely different in Flin Flon," says Paul Rimstead, "is the attitude. Education? Phooey. If a kid played for Flin Flon, he'd quit school. He'd be a pro. He'd work four hours a day underground in the mine and practice. In fact, the school board would not even accept a player in high school. For one thing, the kid would be away on a bus all the time.

"In 1968–69, though, the schools gave in a little. They took one player. The principal at the high school said the player was a test case, and he didn't do badly."

Flin Flon couldn't have cared less what outsiders thought. The town wanted a team and the mine made certain that it had a team. After all, hockey and Josiah Flintabbatey Flonatin made the town famous. Likewise, the Clarkes realized that while it would be nice for their son to continue school, they also were pragmatic about the situation.

"It came down to this," Mrs. Clarke states. "By the time Bobby was 17, he was going to the rink more than he was going to school."

In 1968–69, Bobby's last year of junior hockey, he played 58 games, scoring 51 goals and 86 assists to once again record a league-leading 137 points. Yet perhaps even more significant were the intangibles he displayed that would one day win him the Hart Trophy as the NHL's most valuable player.

"His leadership qualities really came forward his last season at Flin Flon," recounts Ginnell, "even in practice. One day a bunch of the guys were goofing off during a scrimmage and that got Bobby good and mad.

" 'I wanna play hockey for a living and you guys are hurting me and the team by not working hard. So, shape up!' he said. And then, he'd work twice as hard as anybody. By setting an example, Bobby made sure everyone fell into line."

The question that now perplexed Ginnell, Clarke and dozens of NHL scouts centered around his rating with the big-league teams. In June 1969 the NHL draft of juniors was to take place at Montreal's Queen Elizabeth Hotel; and it would only take one day to determine the rest of Bobby Clarke's career. If the moguls believed that a diabetic was a player to avoid, he might just as well get a job in the mine. If somebody showed faith in the 20-year-old with the bright smile, well, there was no telling how high he might climb.

Bobby did not know it at the time but there were some hockey people who believed in him. One of them was Sam Pollock, managing director of the 1969 Stanley Cup champion Montreal Canadiens and perhaps the shrewdest wheeler-dealer in pro hockey. Some of his scouts had rated Clarke as high as number three on their lists. Pollock knew he wasn't going to draft the diabetic on the first round but he definitely wanted him the second time around.

Gerry Melnyk wanted Clarke a little more than Pollock. Melnyk, a former journeyman forward in the NHL, had become an administrative assistant in the Flyers' front office and was regarded as a man with an Argus eye for potentially gifted young stickhandlers. He made his views known to general manager Bud Poile and also advised Poile that Clarke was a diabetic.

Poile decided that, no matter how enthused Melnyk might be about the kid, he wasn't going to draft a questionable hockey product unless the club physician flashed the green light. Without hesitation, Poile went to a phone booth and dialed Dr. Stanley Spoont at Lankenau Hospital in Philadelphia.

"We have this diabetic hockey player we're thinking of drafting," said Poile. "What's your thinking on his chances in the NHL?"

The doctor wasn't going to be glib about it. He needed more information about the boy. "What kind of living habits does he have? Does he take medical advice readily? Is he cooperative?"

Poile didn't have all the answers but his aides did. He conferred with them quickly and returned to the telephone. "Our reports say that he is a very cooperative individual."

That was enough for Dr. Spoont. "Then there is no reason not to take him." He pointed out that other diabetics had reached the top in sports; aces such as Bill Talbert in tennis and Phillies' outfielder Bill Nicholson.

Now the draft was on and Melnyk continued lobbying for the Flyers to pick Clarke in the first round. Melnyk was overruled and Philadelphia selected Robert "Bob" Currier, a 6'1", 190-pound center and right wing who had played for the Cornwall Royals in the Quebec Junior Hockey League.

Melnyk was furious (Currier turned out to be a flop in the Flyers' farm system. He missed part of the 1971–72 season with torn knee ligaments and collected only 40 points in his first four seasons of minor pro hockey). "I'd like to forget that we picked Currier first," Melnyk recalls. "But let's say there were some voices raised at our table."

The selections continued and, finally, the first round ended without anyone plucking Clarke. "If you don't draft Bobby," Melnyk warned his colleagues, "my judgment isn't worth a damn."

NHL President Clarence Campbell announced that the 17th pick was to be made. It was the Philadelphia Flyers' second choice. Assistant general manager Keith Allen now supported Melnyk. "Look," said Allen, "if the guy is available, let's take him."

Just before the Flyers made their move, Sam Pollock walked over to the Philadelphia table and suggested a deal "that you fellows can't refuse" for the Flyers' 17th pick, which would be Clarke. The Flyers refused and Bobby Clarke became Philadelphia's second choice for 1969.

Jimmy Skinner, the portly head scout of the Detroit Red Wings, got up from his chair and conferred with the Flyers' brass. Allen shook his head and shook it a second time. "Skinner told me," Allen comments, "that he'd give us a couple of pros for Clarke. I knew he realized he had made a mistake not picking Bobby ahead of us."

Just how big a mistake remained to be seen. After all, it *is* a long way from Flin Flon to Philadelphia.

3/

Struggling for the Limelight

Leaving his Flin Flon security blanket was not an easy move for Bobby Clarke. He revered his home town as much as *Reminder* publisher Tom Dobson. He would miss Main Street, the nine-hole golf course, the movie house, and the Royal Hotel. Flin Flon may be a pile of rock, but it does have a heart.

Still, there was a living to be made and Bobby reported to the Philadelphia Flyers' training camp at Quebec City that September of 1969 to justify the faith that Pat Ginnell, Gerry Melnyk, and the Flyers' front office had in him.

Not surprisingly, some people at the Spectrum suffered lingering doubts about the decision. "It was a gamble," acknowledges ex-club president Bill Putnam. "We discussed the boy for days. But we felt he was the best young player in Canada, and when our doctors assured us that—under a watchful eye—he could stand up to the grind, we grabbed him. Actually, we wanted him so bad we'd have taken him on the first round if we had to."

At training camp coach Vic Stasiuk placed Bobby on a

line with garrulous veteran Reg Fleming and another promising rookie, Lew Morrison. Clarke played so well that Philadelphia had no choice but to keep him.

However, those who were close to Clarke at the Quebec City camp realized that it wasn't as easy as simply appearing on the ice. There was, as feared, a diabetes scare. Clarke twice passed out and the brass that warned against picking him began second-guessing the Bobby lobby.

For a few days there was some question about whether the strain and grind of NHL play might just not be too much for the diabetic. Then it was learned that Clarke had suffered one of his rare lapses in vigilance, a discovery made by trainer Frank Lewis.

"Both attacks followed morning workouts," said Lewis, "when Bobby had skipped breakfast. If there's one thing an athlete needs, diabetic or not, it's a good, solid breakfast. But Bobby knows now that we've got to be frank with each other and work together on this thing."

As always, Bobby seemed the one least concerned about his ailment. Thoughtful fans wondered and worried about the fact that diabetics often are highly susceptible to infection. Considering that hockey players suffer an inordinate number of cuts and bruises, wasn't he taking a big chance?

"I've been carved up all over the face," says Clarke. "Once, I needed 15 stitches around my eye, but I was back the next game. The attacks I suffered in Quebec City were my first in two or three years."

Following the fainting spells, Lewis and Clarke worked out a regimen. Prior to the match, Bobby would sip a coke with two or three tablespoons of sugar. Between periods he would drink half a glass of sweetened orange juice and after the game, a full glass.

"He doesn't like chocolate bars at game time," Lewis explains, "because they make him thirsty. But I have them in my training kit anyway. I also have a tube of 100 percent glucose which I'm supposed to force down his throat in case of emergency."

As the 1969–70 season progressed without further difficulties, the Flyers' front office began breathing easier and Clarke's critics weren't heard from again. "As his career goes along," observes Dr. Spoont, "he'll be a source of inspiration to diabetics everywhere. I'm really optimistic about this. We've got a tiger by the tail and we can control the tail, so to speak."

The Flyers had also latched on to a superb individual. Clarke's innate goodness soon became legendary around the Spectrum. He was admired not merely because he was a good, young hockey player but also a genuinely sensitive and extremely thoughtful young man.

Once, word got around the Flyers that the daughter of assistant trainer Warren Elliot required a serious heart operation. Elliot needed some financial help if the operation was going to be performed. At just about the same time Bobby was voted "Player Of The Month" by the Flyers Fan Club, for which he also received a cash prize.

Bobby returned the money to fan club president Lou Damia and asked that it be given to Warren Elliot for his daughter's operation. Typically, Clarke did not want any fuss or fanfare made over his generosity but, inevitably, he was asked and prodded about it until he finally explained, "I never met Warren's daughter. I only know what I heard about her problem. The word was that she was young and needed an operation. Warren never told me himself but I wouldn't expect him to. He's not that sort of person.

"I know my small contribution won't pay for the operation, but it will help. He's our assistant trainer and I don't think he makes a fortune. That kind of operation will cost a lot and I know he can use the money more than me."

Elliot, of course, was extremely grateful but not so very surprised, considering the source. "That sort of gratitude makes you feel good," says the assistant trainer. "Bobby's that sort of boy, though. He's completely unselfish. You can't say enough good things about a kid like that."

A lot of good things were being said about Bobby as his rookie season progressed. *Sports Illustrated,* for one, ran a banner headline about the kid from Flin Flon: "PHILLY TAKES A FLYER ON A ROOKIE WITH A HEART." The local papers in Philadelphia liked him just as much, particularly for his Huckleberry Finn manner. And, naturally, Flyers' president Bill Putnam was delighted because the Flyers were drawing bigger crowds than ever before. It confirmed his early prediction that the Flyers would become money-makers within three years.

"Philadelphia," comments Putnam, "is a good sports town and always has been. When I looked around and saw cities like Detroit and Boston and Chicago playing hockey to 96 percent of capacity there was no doubt in my mind that we could make it go in Philadelphia, where we can draw on almost five million people."

The Flyers never did make the playoffs in Clarke's rookie season and Bobby was, deservedly, beaten out for the Calder Memorial Trophy by Chicago Black Hawks' goalie Tony

Esposito. It was not the best of years, nor was it the worst for Clarke.

He played in all 76 games, indicating that his diabetic condition was not a deterrent to heavy playing duties, but scored only 15 goals and 31 assists for 46 points; not exactly the terror of the Goaltenders' Union.

But nobody was complaining at the Spectrum, least of all the ill-advised scouts who had recommened Bob Currier as the Flyers' first draft pick over Clarke in June 1969. Currier played 51 games for the Philadelphia farm team in Quebec City of the American League and scored one goal and four assists for five points.

"Currier is a pretty good hockey player," states Flyers' chief scout Alex Davidson, in defense of the first pick. "A lot of people are asking us about him. The main difference between him and Clarke is that Clarke played in a tougher amateur league and is more advanced than Currier.

"Watch. Currier will be up with the Flyers in a year or two, when he gets the experience he needs. I'm not saying he'll be better than Clarke, but he'll be a pretty good one. Still we're lucky Clarke was available on the second round of that 1969 draft."

For Bobby Clarke, the 1970–71 season can be capsulized in one game, a game between the Flyers and the Stanley Cup champion Boston Bruins. It was going to be a terribly tough contest for the Philadelphians and owner Ed Snider knew it as well as his players. "You guys beat Boston," said Snider before the game, "and I'll buy every one of you *two* new suits."

But the Bruins were the super team of hockey at the time and even though the Flyers played their hearts out, they lost to the better club. This was small solace to Clarke, however, who had scored two goals and seemed to be on the ice all 60 minutes.

At the final buzzer, Clarke dropped his head like a wounded warrior and clambered off to the dressing room. "He tried to keep his head down so the fans near the runway wouldn't see it," wrote Maury Levy in *Philadelphia Magazine*. "But it was hard to hide. Bobby Clarke was crying like a baby."

The fans who did see him tried to shout encouragement. "We'll get 'em next time, Bobby." Yet Bobby kept walking until he was out of sight. He had been trying to carry the Flyers single-handedly and on this night he believed that he had failed.

"A lot of people put their faith in Bobby Clarke," Levy added, "and, in his head, he let them down. Bobby Clarke hung his head low. His curly hair was mussed and dripping and his eyes were burning red."

It was that way at season's end. Thanks to Clarke's 27 goals and 36 assists Philadelphia finished third in 1970–71 but they were wiped right out of the Stanley Cup playoffs in four straight games by the Chicago Black Hawks.

His 63 total points marked a 17-point gain over the previous year and suggested that he would become a substantial scorer in years to come. "The big thing," says Bobby, "is that my all-around play improved as well as my statistics. But I'm not satisfied. I don't think a player should be. Though I've learned a lot, I'm learning more every time out." And Bobby continued to play down the importance of his diabetes. "There are no problems," he would tell people. "I have to do some things. Other players have to do other things. Some have bad backs or bad knees. Some play with plates in their skulls. I don't feel unusual in any way."

He was, of course, unusual and Dr. Spoont and trainer Lewis watched Bobby like a hawk. "There are several ways in which diabetes can affect an athlete," notes Dr. Spoont. "First, if his blood sugar is not normal, his immediate performance is affected. If the blood sugar is too low, for example, he would act peculiar, as though he had lost his coordination. He might have a fainting spell or a convulsion on the ice.

"If his blood sugar was too high, this would also affect his activity, in that muscles would not perform well. It would almost be like he was skating with lead on his feet. The skates would be very heavy for him. As a matter of fact, there are times when Bobby out there looks like his sugar is not right, but usually it's normal. This is a credit to him in the sense that he pushes himself so hard he sometimes just drags himself over the bench. But he is not in any grave danger."

The danger was felt by the enemy goaltenders. Because in 1971–72, Clarke achieved full-fledged stardom. The kid from Flin Flon scored 35 goals and 46 assists for 81 points and he made Philadelphians scream and cry. Now, at the age of 22, he *was* carrying a whole hockey team on his 5′ 10″, 180-pound frame.

For the first time there was general acclaim for Bobby throughout the NHL. On June 7, 1972, he was voted the Bill Masterton Memorial Trophy as the player "who best exemplifies the qualities of perseverance, sportsmanship and dedication to hockey." The kid from Flin Flon, who had set a team record of goals and assists, had become the first Flyer ever to win one of hockey's major trophies.

It was left to Flyers' coach Fred Shero to put him in the proper Philadelphia perspective. "Bobby Clarke," Shero stated, "could possibly be the greatest player in hockey today."

There were many who believed that Shero, at the very least, was being both presumptuous and premature; but the events that would unfold in the months from September 1972 through May 1973 would prove him an uncanny seer.

4/

Bobby vs. the Russians

Perhaps the most revolutionary development since the vulcanized rubber puck hit the ice took place in September 1972 when an eight-game series was arranged between the Soviet National Hockey Club and a group of NHL stars playing under the banner of Team Canada.

For more than two decades the Russians had dominated the international hockey scene and thirsted for competition against the top professionals in North America. But a combination of petty politics and the reluctance of the NHL to expose its aces—and, perish the thought—lose to the Russians made it seem as if the great confrontation would never take place.

Curiously, the sudden emergence of the baby World Hockey Association proved the necessary catalyst for the NHL to soften its stand toward the Russians. The WHA announced almost immediately after birth that it would seek to arrange international games with teams from Czechoslovakia, Sweden, Finland, and, of course, the Soviet Union.

Although the threat seemed hollow at first, the NHL was

not about to take any chances. If any hockey players were going to meet the best of the Russians it would, by God, be the NHL stickhandlers; a fact that was made abundantly clear to the Soviet hockey leaders.

Likewise, the Russians were becoming bored with their endless victories over the quasi-amateur champions of Europe and believed that they had progressed enough to finally go head-on against the major leaguers from the other side of the ocean. Once Soviet officials declared their willingness to cut through the red tape, the NHL flashed its green light and the series was on amid the blare of trumpets and flourish of the speechmakers.

"The prestige of having taken part in these games is something that will last for a lifetime," said NHL President Clarence Campbell. "This could be the beginning of a great and lasting event in sport. In a few years the European champion will be playing the NHL champion for the Stanley Cup."

A series blueprint called for four games in Canada opening in Montreal, then Toronto, Winnipeg, and Vancouver. The teams then would jet to Russia and play the remaining four games in Moscow. Team Canada named former Boston Bruins coach Harry Sinden to head its club with former Montreal Canadiens' left wing John Ferguson as his *aide de camp*.

One of Sinden's first choices for Team Canada was the kid from Flin Flon, Bobby Clarke. Others included Phil Esposito, Dennis Hull, Vic Hadfield, Frank Mahovlich, Rick Martin, Brad Park, Ron Ellis, Paul Henderson, Serge Savard, Yvan Cournoyer, Gary Bergman, Rod Gilbert, Jean Ratelle, Ken Dryden, Tony Esposito and J. P. Parise.

Anticipation for the classic was at a fever pitch. Here was

25

to be the long-awaited test of the big powers. The Russians would pit their radar-passing, wrist-shooting, skate-skate-skate game against the booming slapshots and heavy body work of the NHL.

"I've always believed," Sinden stated, "you should shoot first and pass later. The Russians feel the opposite. So we should see one hell of a contrast.

"As for our strategy, I'll expect our team to adopt the same attitude we encouraged in Phil Esposito when he came to Boston. We told him we had no Bobby Hulls, so he'd have to do his own scoring.

"We've got the best goaltending in the world, so it figures that if we outshoot them, we'll be stressing our advantage. We've got shooters who can score from anywhere between the blue line and center ice."

Listening to Team Canada's officials, observers got the impression that the Russians would be soundly trounced in eight consecutive games. Only a few conceded perhaps a game or two to the newcomers but, confident or not, Sinden knew he had to work to get his players into condition by September 2, 1972.

While Team Canada conducted its pre-series workouts at Maple Leaf Gardens in Toronto, Sinden enjoyed the first and most significant brainstorm. He placed Bobby Clarke at center on a line with Toronto right wing Ron Ellis and left wing Paul Henderson.

A headline in *The Toronto Star* of August 30 said it all: "CLARKE CLICKS WITH PAIR OF LEAFS."

Star reporter Frank Orr was among the first to spot the superior play of the unit. "Clarke, Ellis, and Henderson," Orr wrote, "have quickly acquired the cohesion of a line which has worked together for several seasons. In Team Canada's scheme they have ranked as the most consistent two-way troika, producing goals and excelling defensively."

Henderson likened Clarke's style to that of his Toronto center, Norm Ullman. "Clarke is much the same as Normie," said Henderson. "He drives hard all the time, forechecking and staying on the puck persistently."

Bobby, in turn, commended his new linemates and added that his adrenaline was flowing faster than he could ever recall. "I haven't been this nervous," commented Bobby, "since the day I got married.

"This is the biggest thing that's ever happened to me in sports. I'm proud to have been given the opportunity to play for something more than money. There's so much more at stake here. We're representing our country and finally getting the chance to prove that we are what we believe we are —the best in the world."

If Bobby was nervous, Sinden was confident about the young Philadelphia center. He had watched him carefully through the scrimmages and marvelled at the manner in which he orchestrated his line.

"The Clarke line," Sinden observed prior to the opening game, "has been the surprise of our training camp. Not that we didn't expect them to do well. It's just that we didn't expect the consistency they've played with. They complement each other, and we lucked into it. All three like to hound the puck. All three can skate. And all three always take care of themselves, so they came to camp in shape."

On the eve of the first game Team Canada was considered a heavy favorite. "We gotta win in eight games," said Al Eagleson, executive director of the NHL Players' Association. To which Team Canada left wing Vic Hadfield added: "Everybody's talking eight straight. No ifs, ands, or buts. Eight straight!"

One dissenting voice in the wilderness of wild claims was heard in Montreal where John Robertson, columnist for *The Montreal Star*, warned that Canadians were overlooking the fact that the Russians were in mint condition for the series while Team Canada was still fat and flabby in too many spots—and far too overconfident.

"We're too arrogant," Robertson noted, "and we're committing the fatal sin of underestimating our opposition. I have this nagging feeling that it's going to cost us."

Few observers in the capacity crowd at the Forum worried Robertson's remarks as Team Canada virtually leaped into a 2–0 lead and barely missed scoring a third goal moments later. The game was going just as the NHL cheerleaders had predicted, all Team Canada.

But the Russians come from strong stock. Backed up against the outer limits of Moscow during World War II, they counterattacked when all seemed lost. And there was a striking similarity in the performance of the Soviet National Hockey Team that night in Montreal.

Down 2–0, their rally took on epic proportions; and when they were through Team Canada conducted a disorderly retreat out of the Forum, beaten 7–3. Nobody was more depressed about the result than Bobby Clarke who believed he had a reasonable explanation for the debacle.

"Maybe this is an excuse," said Bobby, "but this was our first game together as a team. They were by far the superior club tonight. It all comes back to conditioning. We were played out. We just couldn't keep up with them.

"The heat was a factor and maybe it bothered us more than them because they're in so much better shape. But they had the puck all night. It's much easier to play with the puck than chasing it."

Like others, Clarke was convinced that Team Canada would be better the second time around. "After two or three games," he went on, "we'll have a better idea of how good they really are. We're disappointed, but we'll come back."

The teams moved on to Toronto for Game Two. In one game the worm had turned and now the NHL aces suddenly found themselves up against the wall. "I think I'll go to church and pray," despaired center Jean Ratelle.

"I'd go with you," kidded Phil Esposito, "but with my luck the place would burn down!"

Prior to Game Two, Bobby Clarke lounged in the lobby of Toronto's Sutton Place Hotel and talked about the Montreal disaster. "One game," he said, "is sure worth at least 20 practices. When you're tired after 30 seconds in a scrimmage you coast for half a minute to regain your breath and then go again. In the games, you can't do that; at least not against the Russians.

"The funny part of it is that the Russians were supposed to be here to learn something from us. Well, we really fooled them, didn't we? They didn't learn a thing from us, except that you have to get in shape. They already know that."

As Clarke predicted, the NHL aces pulled themselves together in time for Game Two and defeated the Russians, 4–1. Yet despite the three-goal margin, the Canadians did not leave the ice overconfident. It was a hard-earned win that, more than anything, served to convince them that the Soviet sextet was as competent as some of the best teams in the

NHL. Any doubts were erased at Winnipeg where the Russians stoutly fought from behind a 1–3 deficit to gain a 4–4 tie.

By this time a sizable number of Canadians had become disillusioned with their team's failure to dominate the series. The players they were watching in person or on television were simply not as good as their press clippings and when the NHL players skated out on Vancouver ice for the fourth game they were stung with thousands of boos from among the 18,000 spectators packed into the Pacific Coliseum.

The boos, for Clarke and his teammates, proved to be one of the most saddening experiences of their respective careers. "We were very disappointed," recalls Bobby. "It's one thing to be booed when you're playing for your own individual team. But it's something else to be booed when you're playing for your country."

The derisive hoots got worse and worse as the game progressed and the Russians skated away to a 5–3 triumph. Russia's amazingly indefatigable skaters thus won the first half of the series two games to one with one tie. Now it was on to the Kremlin for Phase Two and the last hope for Team Canada to salvage respect in the hockey world.

From a purely personal viewpoint, Bobby Clarke was immensely pleased with himself. His perseverance and grim determination on the ice had won plaudits from critics who had otherwise been extremely harsh with the NHL stars. In his heart, Bobby knew that he had taken a giant step toward stardom.

"My confidence was reinforced quite a bit," he admits. "Before I played with the guys from Team Canada, I wasn't sure I really belonged on the ice with them. I was always in awe of people like Phil Esposito and Brad Park. But once we got on the ice together I became much more confident and pretty soon I felt I could play as well as the rest of them."

Game One in Moscow, on September 22, 1972, was a nightmare for Team Canada in general and Bobby Clarke in particular. The NHL aces lost a 4–1 lead and found themselves tied, 4–4, when Clarke tried to control a bouncing puck along the boards. He finally sent it back to his friend and roommate, Rod Seiling of the Rangers. Unfortunately, Seiling never got the puck.

"It was a bad play," Bobby later lamented. "What guy in his right mind passes the puck back to somebody deep in his own zone at that stage of the game? I don't think the puck ever got to Rod."

But it did get to Valery Kharlamov who passed it to his teammate Vladimir Ivanovich Vikulov who deposited the rubber behind Team Canada goalie Tony Esposito. The goal won the game, 5–4.

Now the Canadians' cause appeared as hopeless as Team Russia's had before the tournament. Hopeless to all, perhaps, but Vsevolod Brobrov, the Soviet coach who deeply respected the ability of the NHL stars.

"The Canadians," said Brobrov, "were not on form in Canada. They had not trained much and they were overconfident. Now they will be stronger. They will take the next games more seriously. And they will be in better condition. They have played more and they are well-motivated."

A key reason for this motivation was their desire to win, not only for the pride of Canada and the NHL but also to show they could survive the defection of Vic Hadfield, Josh Guevremont, Richard Martin, and Gil Perreault who left

Team Canada and returned home, pouting because they did not get enough ice time. This was the decisive moment. Either the NHL players would allow the mission to fall apart or they would pull themselves together and play the best hockey of their lives. Boston Bruins' center Phil Esposito proved to be the unifying force and titular head of the players.

Esposito tongue-lashed his mates into thinking victory while coach Sinden developed a passionate feeling among the skaters. He denounced those who had left the club as "rats" that had jumped ship and urged the remaining players to give the Russians their best in the final three games.

The Sinden–Esposito combination worked and in Game Six Team Canada squeaked past the Russians, 3–2. This meant the NHL aces still had a chance to win the series, provided they won Games Seven and Eight. Impossible? No. Difficult, yes!

A lot of the folks back home had lowered their horizons. Dreams of an eight-game sweep were of the past. All they wanted now were a pair of wins and the Canadians said so in an astonishing outpouring of telegrams to their heroes. More than 50,000 rooters, from Nova Scotia to British Columbia, sent cheering wires. Needless to say, some of them came from Flin Flon, Manitoba. "I knew they wouldn't forget me," Clarke said with a smile.

Nor did Team Canada forget how to win. For more than two-and-a-half periods the clubs battled evenly; and now in Game Seven, with less than three minutes remaining, the scoreboard read Team Canada 3, USSR 3. Then, Clarke's linemate Paul Henderson split the Russian defense and beat goalie Vladislav Tretiak. Final score: Team Canada 4, USSR 3. The series was tied, 3–3–1.

Game Eight has justifiably been called one of the most extraordinary hockey exhibitions since Lord Stanley of Preston donated a Cup to stickhandlers at the turn of the century. With millions of fans watching on television or listening on radio, the unofficial world championship was at stake.

At first it appeared that the superbly conditioned Russians, playing on their home rink, would prevail. They led, 5–3, with two minutes elapsed in the third period and appeared to be in command until Phil Esposito rallied the team. He beat Tretiak with a close-in shot at 2:27 to pull Canada to within a goal of tying the score. At 12:56 Esposito's pass put fleet Yvan Cournoyer in the clear and the squat Canadien fired the puck into the net bringing all of North America to its feet.

The Russian defense tightened. A tie would be just fine for the Soviets and they appeared capable of getting it as the clock ticked past the 19-minute mark. Coach Sinden had hoped to send out a fresh unit: the line of Clarke, Henderson, and Ellis. However, only Henderson was able to get onto the ice since Esposito was in control of the puck.

Moving toward the Soviet net, Esposito shot from a difficult angle. Tretiak made the save but allowed the puck to rebound free. Henderson was there to drill the rubber low and to the right. Tretiak sprawled and extended his left glove to the corner. But too late. The puck was in. Team Canada won, 6–5!

For Bobby Clarke it was an unforgettable experience. He had helped glue Team Canada together in its early trying days and his effervescence later served as an inspiration to the seasoned veterans. He learned from his colleagues and he learned from his opponents.

"The Russians proved to me that they really are great hockey players," said Clarke. "Personally, I'd like to play them again. Whether I do or not, the series in September 1972 will never be forgotten; particularly the games in Moscow. I really felt I was playing for our national honor."

Bobby returned home and rejoined the Philadelphia Flyers. He may not have been aware of it at the time but starting in October 1972 he would be waging a more personal battle; one whose results would have a long-term effect on hockey in Philadelphia.

5/

Bobby vs. Derek

When Bobby Clarke returned from Moscow to Philadelphia he encountered a city conspicuously lacking in brotherly love when it came to professional ice hockey. For the first time since the Quakers and the Arrows vied for attention in 1930, Philadelphians were given the opportunity of supporting two professional hockey teams.

The new team in town was the World Hockey Association's entry: the Blazers. Considered by many to be the WHA's most powerful club, the Blazers had a spate of former NHL skaters. Player–coach was John McKenzie, the oft-booed Boston Bruin. Other big-leaguers included André Lacroix, a former favorite with the Flyers, Bryan "Soupy" Campbell, and goaltender Bernie Parent who was once considered as much a part of the Philadelphia landscape as Independence Hall.

But Parent had declared his independence from the NHL during the Winter of 1971–72 and signed with the Miami Screaming Eagles of the WHA. When the Eagles were grounded, Parent's contract was absorbed by the Blazers and

Bernie promised to give them the kind of goaltending worthy of the NHL's best.

Important as these WHA acquisitions may have been, they all added up to small potatoes compared with the gala signing of former Boston Bruins' center Derek Sanderson to a multi-year, multi-million dollar contract. Now, it appeared to some well-informed hockey-watchers, the Flyers were in trouble.

As everyone from Broad Street to Penn Station knew, Derek's middle name was Charisma. He had been featured, semi-nude, in color, in bed as part of a *Life* magazine spread. His autobiography, *I've Got To Be Me*, was a best-seller. He was the first hockey player to go mod and wear a mustache. And, besides that, he was good.

To the instant delight of the Philadelphia media, Derek never stopped talking. He seemed happy to be a part of the Pennsylvania hockey scene. "I've always lived like a millionaire," Derek boasted. "Now I can afford it. I bought a town house in Society Hill and got a Rolls-Royce that only cost $31,000."

Sanderson's patron saint throughout his early career as a Blazer was James L. Cooper, a 42-year-old attorney who served as chairman of the Atlantic National Bank in Atlantic City, New Jersey. Cooper admittedly was a sports fan and revelled in the publicity both he and Sanderson were attracting away from the Flyers.

"All I know," said Cooper, "is that our league and the NHL can survive and succeed independently."

The answer would be supplied at the turnstiles. Sanderson, for all his talk, was not selling Blazers' season tickets at the brisk pace Cooper had hoped; nor were Parent, Lacroix, Campbell, et al. But it was still too soon to tell. On Friday night, October 13, 1973, the Blazers would open the doors of a rejuvenated Civic Center and, hopefully, 9000 seats would be filled.

Despite all the fuss and fanfare of an expensive publicity campaign, only 5000 people turned out to see Philadelphia's newest professional team. Or at least so they hoped.

What they saw was a travesty on professional sports' promotion. The game was never held because the ice was so poor it cracked under the ice-cleaning machine. "It was so bad, the Blazers' debut," wrote John Brogan in *The Bulletin*, "that even his own worst enemies had to feel for Jim Cooper."

The game was officially postponed. Still, the embarrassment lingered on. "It's bad," Cooper said. "We created a lot of ill-will out there."

But nothing compared to the ill-will Sanderson would soon create. His target, not surprisingly, was the Flyers and, at last, Bobby Clarke. First, however, Derek decided to defend the opening night fiasco; if that were possible. "It was bad," Derek conceded, "but no worse than when the roof blew off the Spectrum."

The Blazers eventually did learn how to make skateable ice but they never could figure out how to lure people into their rink. For in no time at all it had become apparent that Sanderson, as a Blazer, had all the charisma of a three-toed sloth.

As a player, his contributions were minimal and then the Blazers suddenly discovered he had been admitted to the hospital, complaining of back problems. While bedridden, Sanderson managed to rap Philadelphia and its sportswriters before he reversed his field to turn his guns on Clarke.

"Listen," said Sanderson, "Clarke works harder than I do. He's fast and he's got a lot of guts; he ain't afraid of nobody. He scores goals and he gives you 110 percent every night. But I'm a better hockey player than Clarke in certain phases of the game."

This gratuitous kick-in-the-pants achieved one goal, if nothing else. It totally nauseated the Flyers' front office, especially manager Keith Allen. "That drives me nuts!" snapped Allen when apprised of Derek's monologue. "What has Sanderson ever done? It's ridiculous. It's not even close. Clarke is the best checker in the league, a great face-off man, a great scorer and a great playmaker. And that's not all: Bobby's a leader; a class guy who sets the example on and off the ice. Hard work is his middle name. The one phase the other guy might be better in, is his mouth."

Flyers' president Ed Snider matched Allen in decibel counts when *he* learned about Sanderson's remarks. "Sanderson," said Snider, "was the fourth-best center in town—behind Clarke, Clement, MacLeish. Or fifth; André Lacroix may be better."

Undaunted, Sanderson resumed his attack. "Humility," added Derek, "has a place in hockey. Go ask Bobby Clarke if he's a better hockey player than I am."

When the question was finally put to Bobby, he was amused. "How can you compare hockey players? Sanderson is a great penalty-killer. He played against the top lines. He didn't get the opportunity to play on the power play that I've had.

"The thing is, he's outspoken. He says he's the best face-off guy in the league. I couldn't say that. We're just different personalities, that's all. And I can't change. If I envied Sanderson I could do the same things. He told writers he had 60 suits when he had six. Anybody can say that. Anybody can get that kind of image. But he's a heckuva hockey player. Him and Mahovlich, they were as tough to play as anyone for me. Aggressive, confident."

At times it was difficult to determine whether Clarke scorned or sympathized with Sanderson. The Flyers' leader seemed to understand Derek better than Derek understood himself. "We're all playing the game for money," Bobby concluded. "It boils down to how much money did he need to be happy? If I wanted more money I could have gone to the other league."

Then, a pause: "Just ask Derek if he's happy in that league."

With each day of inactivity, Sanderson seemed more and more unhappy. His absence from the Blazers' lineup caused raised eyebrows because he appeared ready to play but the Blazers weren't playing him. In addition, several of the Philadelphia writers—especially Frank Dolson of *The Inquirer* and Maury Levy of *Philadelphia Magazine*—were on Derek with a vengeance. Dolson made it a policy never to mention Derek by name. Levy placed Sanderson first on his list of "35 People I Can Do Without."

One by one anti-Sanderson stories began to surface until he had achieved the status of the black sheep of Philadelphia sports. This became apparent to the Blazers whose owner, Bernard Brown, engaged Sanderson in a contract dispute. By now Sanderson wanted to get back on the ice but the Blazers didn't wish any part of him. Attorneys for both sides entered the case and, eventually, a separation agreement was arranged.

On February 7, 1973, Sanderson signed a new contract with the Boston Bruins. The Battle of Philadelphia had been won by Bobby Clarke and the Flyers.

6/
The Mean Machine Makes the Playoffs

The contrast between Bobby Clarke and the Flyers' Mean Machine was like the difference between a Boy Scout and the Dead End Kids. A Madison Avenue advertising agency couldn't have dreamt up a more appealing personality than young Bobby. Yet though he was the acknowledged leader of his team, Bobby resented the rising tide of stories that depicted him as the Saviour of the Spectrum. "We aren't losers anymore; and I think one reason is that we don't depend upon any one player. We take turns leading. That's the way a good team does it."

His modesty notwithstanding, Clarke could not deny his accomplishments which were immense during the 1972–73 season. For example, during a game against the Montreal Canadiens at the Forum, Philadelphia came away with a 7–6 victory. Bobby scored a three-goal hat trick; the winning goal achieved with only 3:39 remaining in the game.

On that last one, Bobby stole the puck from Canadiens' defenseman Bob Murdoch and battled his way to the right, stickhandling and grappling past Montreal's ace backliner, Jacques Laperriere. This flurry forced Bobby to turn away from the net, yet somehow he found the bouncing puck and sliced a shot past All-Star goalie Ken Dryden. Even partisan Montrealers agreed that the kid from Flin Flon was Hart Trophy (most valuable player) material and Flyers' manager Keith Allen was not disinclined to agree.

"In Philadelphia," Allen observed, "there's nobody but Clarke to consider. Rick MacLeish has had a remarkable year, but I'd hate to think where the Flyers would be without Clarke." Together with his diabetes, Bobby also has a little difficulty with his eyesight which is 200–100 myopic. "That means," he explains, "trouble seeing far away. I never wore lenses in Junior hockey. If I'm on top of the play, I'm okay. It's when the puck is in the air that I have trouble judging it."

Yet Clarke would still be the All-Canadian Boy, except for one factor: the company he was keeping. By the middle of the 1972–73 season the Broad Street Bullies had established themselves as the riotous swashbucklers of the NHL. Their scorn for the rulebook was notorious from Flin Flon to Toronto and a cause for alarm at NHL headquarters in Montreal.

"They are the hockey equivalent of the Flyer who would strafe lifeboats," said *Toronto Globe and Mail* columnist Dick Beddoes. "They should play in spiked helmets. You get a picture, after the Flyers demolished the Minnesota North Stars, of a guy coming up to them and saying, 'Did you beat Minnesota?' and the Flyers answering, 'Yeah, and we also burned down Minneapolis'."

Inevitably Clarke would be affected by the brawlers around him. For like Gordie Howe who once defended hockey violence by asserting that "It *is* a man's game," Clarke too is aware.

"The overall play of our team helped each player individually," Bobby said. "I found that I was left alone more than in the past because anytime someone bothered me, someone on the Flyers went after him."

It happened during a game against Detroit. Big defenseman Gary Bergman of the Red Wings grappled with Clarke and, in a trice, Bill Barber and Bill Flett of the Flyers rushed to his aid like firemen responding to an alarm. "That's the difference between the teams," comments Bobby. "Two guys helped me and nobody helped Bergman."

Philadelphia's no-holds-barred bulldozing style caused tremors in Detroit, tantrums in Toronto, and a riot in Vancouver as the Flyers added hour upon hour of penalties to their record. By season's end they had accumulated an NHL standard for penalties—1,754 minutes, which was cause for lobbying by several of the team's sworn enemies.

Eventually the anti-Flyers' faction developed a high enough decibel count to reach NHL President Clarence Campbell's ears. The league czar shook a warning finger in the direction of Flyers' manager Allen. The NHL's position was that the Flyers seemed to be intimidating—or, at least trying to intimidate—referees and linesmen as well as enemy skaters.

"I warned him," said Campbell, "that action would be taken and I have the authority to suspend him. When you continually attack the officials you are attacking the structure of the league."

To which Allen categorically replied: "We're not going to change our style of play."

As for Bobby Clarke, he believed his mates were being victimized by generalization and the media's tendency to exaggerate a "good" story; in this case the blustery bullies from Broad Street. It was true the Flyers loved to fight but they also scored lots of goals and they finished right behind the Chicago Black Hawks in the West Division race.

"We finished second," said Clarke. "You have to have some good hockey players to do that. Everybody has built us up to be just a rough team. Dummies. It's not so. And I don't think intimidation is a factor. Not in the playoffs. Hitting, yes, but not intimidation."

By playoff time, 1973, Bobby Clarke had fulfilled the promise of his September press clippings when he surprised everyone in the Team Canada camp. He finished second in the scoring race behind perennial leader Phil Esposito with 37 goals and 67 assists for 104 points in 78 games.

While many of his Team Canada colleagues such as Paul Henderson, Ron Ellis, and Gary Bergman suffered through mediocre campaigns after the pulsating Russian series, Bobby never missed a beat. And, while he himself never made much of it, he *did* help knock Derek Sanderson and the Blazers right out of Philadelphia.

"I think," said Clarke, "that the only ones we helped were ourselves. I didn't give Sanderson much thought; I have my own problems. What he did worked out for him financially but it sure gave him a lousy image. And he didn't play well in 1972–73 either. I guess it all depends on what you're looking for. If he was just after financial success, he seems to have gotten it."

Bobby had been to the playoffs before, but only briefly. He was an NHL sophomore on the Philadelphia sextet that was wiped out of the series by Chicago in four straight games. "I played against Stan Mikita," he remembers. "I touched the puck maybe three times a game."

His record indicated as much. Bobby scored no goals and no assists for no points; just two penalty minutes. Now he was back at the well, thirstier than ever for playoff glory. Philadelphia's first opponent would be the Minnesota North Stars and in Game One at the Spectrum it looked, for a moment, as though Clarke might never play hockey again.

A teammate's stick accidentally nicked his right eye. Bobby fell to the ice face down, his legs banging like a baby's to express the pain. Dr. Stanley Spoont, the team physician, rushed to his side.

"I can't see! I can't see!" Bobby cried.

The cornea had been scratched. The stick had broken Bobby's hard contact lens. Two fragments of lens were under the lid of his eye. Dr. Spoont calmed him. "It's like a boxer who gets punched in the eye," the doctor later explained. "After a couple of minutes he was able to see and we walked him to the clubhouse."

A police escort rushed Clarke to the hospital where an eye specialist removed the lens fragments. "He was in pain," said Dr. Spoont. "They gave him ointment and they thought it would clear up. He woke up the next morning and his eye was so sore that he said there was no way he could put anything in it, but the soft contact lenses worked."

Then, Dr. Spoont explained the special quality about Clarke that marks him above the others. "His arm could be dangling at his side and he'd play. He's an amazing competitor. I worry about him any time he's cut because diabetics don't always heal fast. But Bobby does."

That night, less than 24 hours after the accident, he went out and played against the bruising North Stars. He didn't score a goal but he was everywhere and the Flyers won the game 4–1 to tie the series at one apiece.

"I couldn't care less if he never scores a goal," said coach Shero. "He does enough to win games for us. Lots of guys can come up with the odd goal and they haven't contributed anything. But if I had 15 Bobby Clarke's the outcome would never be in doubt."

"I knew he'd play," defenseman Joe Watson affirmed. "He's that kind of guy. He means as much to us as Bobby Orr and Phil Esposito mean to the Bruins. The guts he shows, everybody else has to give 100 percent. Him, he gives 150."

The eye injury bothered Clarke, to be sure, but not enough to keep him from leading the Flyers to a first round victory over Minnesota. "I'd have gone out there with no glasses," he said, "and no lenses. I'd have wanted to play as long as I could help the team . . . take faceoffs or something."

He now had to help the team against the Montreal Canadiens. It would be his biggest challenge since Moscow. Bobby skated against Henri "Pocket Rocket" Richard, the galvanic captain of the Canadiens. Henri had been to the Stanley Cup well many times before and tasted the champagne. If there was a playoff trick in the book, Henri knew it; and then some. He threw everything he had at Clarke and Bobby came away filled with admiration.

"Henri," said Clarke, "is always there. Every time I pick up the puck he's coming at me from somewhere. He's been hit quite a few times; by me, by our defense, but he doesn't stop. It's frustrating when you outweigh a guy by 20 pounds, knock him down and he's up and gone before you are."

They were playing for all the marbles, the winner to move on to the finals. In time, sticks were raised and wounds were opened. The image of Bobby Clarke, the Boy Scout, had changed. He was playing the Montreal captain as tough as possible, his stick frequently around Richard's eyes.

"I don't think I played dirty," Bobby asserted, "and I don't think Henri thought I played dirty. I did cut his face once, but it wasn't intentional. It just happened. I got cut a few times myself. I don't think I've changed my style at all. I'm not a rough player."

The Canadiens militantly disagreed. After the fourth game of the series, hard-nosed Jim Roberts of Montreal limped about the dressing room with a bandage on one thigh. "I got that courtesy of Mr. Clean (Clarke) and his knee. Hell, Clarke gives it to you whenever he makes contact," he said.

In that same match, which the Canadiens won 4–1 to take a three games to one series lead, Clarke antagonized other Canadiens. Red Burnett, who has been covering hockey for *The Toronto Star* a good many years, was less than charitable in evaluating Bobby's style. Burnett called Clarke, "the man with the choirboy smile and educated knees, elbows and stick."

Some Montreal players contended that Clarke's image helped him obtain leniency from the referees. In the fourth game of the semi-finals Clarke mauled Henri Richard and escaped without punishment from the officials. "Bobby cut me for six stitches on the head," said Richard. "I'm sure the referee saw it but there was no penalty. Later, some Flyer lifted Larry Robinson's (Montreal defenseman) stick and it

47

nicked Clarke for two stitches. We got a five-minute major penalty."

Whatever their tactics, neither Clarke nor his teammates could solve the Canadiens. For in five games they were eliminated from the semi-finals by Montreal, the eventual Stanley Cup winners. On paper it didn't appear to be a very close series, but in their hearts the Canadiens knew differently. Certainly, the Philadelphia Faithful never embraced a club more warmly than when the Flyers returned from Montreal.

"Bobby Clarke's Comeback Kids never wavered in making the Canadiens, hockey's best team, dig deep for every goal," wrote Bill Fleischman in *The Daily News.* "From outcasts to semi-finalists in one year—a proud accomplishment."

7/

End of the Rainbow

If anyone had suggested to Philadelphia Flyers' boss Ed Snider that the 17th player claimed in the 1969 amateur draft would, in May 1973, be selected for the Hart Trophy as the NHL played adjudged the most valuable to his team it is quite possible that Snider would have tumbled from his chair laughing.

Yet, in September 1969, while the Flyers' first-year men were working out at Le Colisée in Quebec City, someone detected that rare quality of utter superiority in just such a man.

"Within three years," said Bud Poile, then general manager of the Flyers, "that 20-year-old boy will be the best in the league. And if he's not the best I'll guarantee you he will be in the top three."

Poile was talking to his heir apparent, Keith Allen, about a rather awkward center named Bobby Clarke. Precisely what it was about Clarke that inspired Poile's raves remains somewhat of a mystery. But as the 1972–73 season winded down to a playoff conclusion it was evident that Poile either knew what he was talking about, or had made an awfully good guess.

By the time the Flyers went up against the Montreal Canadiens in April 1973 Bobby had irrevocably become Mister Hockey in Philadelphia. Such veterans as Ed Van Impe, an original Flyer, knew it as well as the man-in-the-street. Players such as forward Terry Crisp, who was new to the team, sensed it immediately upon entering the Flyers' dressing room.

"He's an amazing player," said Crisp. "He does so much, so well. And there's his desire to win. Plus what may be his greatest asset, the way he meets people. He keeps the image of the hockey player alive at a time when you hear cries of brutality and animals. It's refreshing to see a guy like Clarke. He skates hard, kills penalties, works the power play. Listen, he'd drive the ice-cleaning machine if they wanted him to."

As always, Bobby became pleasantly disputatious when informed of the compliments. Why him? That was his standard response. When it was suggested early in May 1973 that Clarke was a candidate for the Hart Trophy he was still surprised. Not when there were titans such as Bobby Orr, Phil Esposito, Frank Mahovlich, and Stan Mikita skating in his midst.

"If the Hart Trophy was given to the best player," commented Clarke, "it would go to Bobby Orr every year, hands down."

By any standard, the Clarke family is as typically American (or Canadian) as it's possible for a hockey superstar's family to be. Sandra Clarke, Bobby's wife, met him while they were neighbors in Flin Flon; and by May 1973 they'd been married for three years and had a 19-month-old son.

"We grew up together," says Mrs. Clarke, "and started dating when I was a cheerleader at the junior games."

Sandra Clarke does not have stars in her eyes, nor does she covet the glamor that surrounds big-name hockey players. This was underscored following Bobby's Team Canada experience when reporter Sandra Peredo of *The Canadian Magazine* asked Sandra Clarke how she liked being the wife of Philadelphia's most adored hockey player.

"People don't understand that you're just a normal person," she replied, "that sometimes you walk around in blue jeans and 'go grubby.' If I'm shopping and I'm recognized and my hair isn't right or something, they just can't believe it."

Bobby and Sandra began dating when he played for the Bombers. Sandra was familiar with the life style of hockey players and their wives, and believed it a good one.

"But," she adds, "it's not really that exciting except at the games, and I find it hard to comprehend why people think we're so different. They come to my door and say, 'Can we look at him?'

"I don't bother living up to any image. If they don't like me the way I am, forget it. It's been much easier since we've had the baby because he keeps me busy and he's company. Before he was born we lived in an apartment and if Bobby was going to be away for four days . . . well, the first day you clean the apartment, and then if you don't really enjoy shopping, you're stuck. You watch television, take a walk.

"Since then we've bought a home and in our time together we don't do anything special. We take the baby out, or now that the pool is frozen we skate on it. I don't think our life is that much different from other people's."

*   *   *

Voting for the Hart Trophy is conducted by the Professional Hockey Writers' Association. And on May 25, 1973, the results for the year were published. Phil Esposito of Boston scored 96 points. His colleague, Bobby Orr, tallied 63. Ken Dryden, goalie for the Stanley Cup champion Montreal Canadiens had 53, and gifted center Gil Perreault of the Buffalo Sabres captured 25 points.

They all were also-rans behind Philadelphia's young center, Bobby Clarke, who scored a landslide victory with 158 points. Bill Brennan, the ubiquitous hockey writer for *The Detroit News*, explained the result as logically as any voter.

"Clarke," said Brennan, "was the heart and soul of the Flyers. When they made him captain in mid-season, it went up and beyond that. As for the runners-up, Phil Esposito is nothing without Bobby Orr, and Montreal kept winning when Ken Dryden was hurt. Clarke scored 104 points with a weaker club."

Bobby did his very best to put in a disclaimer but it was too late. "I don't know how they picked me as most valuable player," he demurred. "We had Rick MacLeish with 50 goals and Bill Flett with 43."

Flyers' owner Ed Snider listened patiently and applauded Bobby's explanation. Now it was Snider's turn and his statement was simplicity and accuracy itself.

Bobby Clarke, the myopic diabetic had dreamed of such a day during his childhood in Flin Flon. But never, in his wildest fantasies, would he dare imagine that it would all come true. Yet, he now had reached the end of the rainbow. He had won the Hart Trophy.

"It is," concluded Snider, "a great day for Bobby Clarke, the Flyers, and Philadelphia!"

11

Hockey in Philadelphia—
How It All Began

8 /

The Quivering Quakers

Although organized amateur hockey was played in Philadelphia as far back as the turn of the century, the professionals didn't make their debut until the Autumn of 1927 when the Philadelphia Arrows were admitted to the powerful Canadian-American League.

One of the foremost minor hockey leagues on the continent, the Can-Am, as it was known, had been organized in 1926 with representatives from New Haven, Springfield, Quebec City, Boston, and Providence.

When the league decided to expand to six teams Philadelphia was granted a franchise for the 1927–28 season and a contest was held by the new entry to select a name. Some 4268 letters later, a panel of sportswriters selected THE ARROWS.

"It was selected," commented *The Philadelphia Evening Ledger*, "because it denotes speed and ice hockey is known to be a speedy game."

But speed appeared to be foreign to the Arrows in their maiden year. They finished dead last and showed no improvement the following season. However, in 1929–30 the Arrows climbed to second place only to be eliminated from the play-offs by Boston.

The team, which had been controlled by an out-of-towner, Irwin P. Wener of New Haven, was taken over by a group of Philadelphians in June 1929. Heading the group of notables was Irwin P. Griscom, III. Associated with Griscom in the purchase of Wener's stock was F. Eugene Dixon, captain of the United States Davis Cup tennis team; George D. Widener, the noted turfman, as well as J. Haseltine Carstairs, John Story Smith, and Alexander Thayer.

Despite the new blood and new money, the Arrows continued to spend their seasons in the lower reaches of the Can-Am. Meanwhile, the seeds of big-league hockey for Philadelphia were being planted—of all places—in Pittsburgh, at the other end of the state.

Prior to the start of the 1928–29 National Hockey League season, Benny Leonard, who had been the lightweight champion of the world, bought the NHL's Pittsburgh franchise and operated it in the Smoky City as THE PIRATES with no financial success.

On October 18, 1930, the NHL Board of Governors approved Leonard's request to move the Pittsburgh franchise to Philadelphia. Ebullient Benny reacted as if he had been granted a license to coin money. He promptly spelled out elaborate plans for the "new" club, renamed THE QUAKERS, and promised Philadelphians a brand new ice palace, which would replace the already antiquated Arena.

"The present building won't be large enough to hold the crowds," Benny boasted. "We are expecting a larger one to be erected three years from now. If it isn't, I intend to bring

New York capital in here and erect a modified Madison Square Garden that will house hockey, six-day bicycle races and wrestling."

Leonard's transplanted Pittsburgh club was nothing to crow about, either artistically or financially. As The Pirates, they finished dead last in the American Division of the NHL during the 1929–30 campaign. Their record of five wins, 36 losses, and three times was generally regarded as the joke of the NHL; it was hardly surprising that one of the leading jokesters on the Pirates was their goaltender—Joe Miller.

Miller accompanied Leonard to Philadelphia but Benny's optimism was not diminished one iota. "I think ice hockey has the greatest future of any sport in America," Leonard predicted. "So I'm willing to risk my money. I've lost plenty so far but I'm not crying. It's the coming sport in Philadelphia and two years from now you'll say I was right."

Leonard's choice as general manager–coach of the Quakers was Cooper Smeaton, a widely respected hockey man who had been referee-in-chief of the NHL at the time of his appointment. Smeaton had been through the hockey wars and was thankful to be alive when Leonard phoned him about the job. Being a referee was not a very safe job in those "frontier" days of pro hockey.

Smeaton had survived a number of close calls. Once, while officiating a match between Ottawa and Quebec in Quebec City, Cooper called several plays against the home club which enraged the already hostile French-Canadian audience.

Ottawa won the game by one goal and Smeaton was generally considered the culprit by the audience, a fact of which the referee was acutely aware. "Lucky for me," said Smeaton, "the referee and linesmen used to share the visiting team's dressing room since we didn't have a changing room of our own. I realized how fortunate I was moments after the final buzzer that night in Quebec."

The hard-nosed, outspoken Smeaton was Leonard's kind of man and served to stoke up more of Benny's enthusiastic fire. "This is a major league operation," Leonard boasted prior to the Quakers' opening game. "The Quakers are to ice hockey what the Athletics (then world champions) are to baseball."

Leonard was half right. He did have a major league operation everywhere but on the ice. His trainer, Archie Campbell, was as big-league as general manager–coach Smeaton. Campbell, after returning from service in World War I, worked for a good many hockey and football teams.

Campbell had been around sports operations a lot longer than Leonard. One look at the Quakers' roster and Archie saw the handwriting on the wall. "Benny knew his hockey," said Campbell, "but I could tell, as far as that team was concerned, he didn't have a chance."

Plain and simple, the Quakers didn't have the talent. Forwards Hibbert "Hib" Milks and Gerald Lowrey were the best of a mediocre lot. Dubious about Joe Miller's goaltending capabilities, Smeaton also signed 21-year-old Welsh-born Wilf Cude. A high-strung personality, Cude spent a horrendous season guarding the Quakers' goal. The experience, no doubt, brought on Cude's premature retirement from the sport in what is regarded as one of the most unusual retirement episodes in the game.

"I was having my afternoon steak before a game," said Cude, "and I poured a helluva lot of catsup on it. I'd just started to eat the steak when my wife, Beulah, made some casual remark about a trivial subject. For no good reason, I picked up my steak and threw it at her.

"She ducked and the steak wound up smacking against the wall. The catsup splattered and the steak hung there on the wall. Slowly it began to slip down and I stared at it. Between the time that steak hit the wall and then hit the floor, I decided I'd had enough of goaltending. When it landed I had made my decision to retire."

Judging by the Quakers' record in their first weeks of operation one could understand Cude's edginess, not to mention Smeaton's. Philadelphia opened the 1930–31 season at the Arena on November 11, 1930, and lost 3–0 to the New York Rangers. They scored only one goal in their first three games, all losing affairs, before tying Ottawa 2–2. A momentous occasion—the Quakers' first victory—took place on November 25, 1930, at the Arena. The Toronto Maple Leafs were beaten, 2–1.

Leonard began to get the message but his enthusiasm still ran high. "We're off to a slow start here this year," he admitted, "but I'm positive that Philadelphians will take to major hockey in another year or two. They have to become educated to it."

Leonard underestimated the Philadelphia fans. They were quite educated and were quick to realize that Benny had assembled what was to become the worst team in big-league hockey history. They did not win a single game from November 29, 1930, to January 10, 1931, and set a league record which still stands, losing 15 consecutive matches.

Somewhat depressed by now but still hopeful, Leonard made a few trades and imported Stan Crosset, a towering defenseman from Port Hope, Ontario. Crossett's experience in the NHL—and one episode in particular—symbolized more than anything the ill-starred life of the Quakers.

The Quakers were in Detroit for a game against the Falcons (later the Red Wings) and Smeaton gathered his men together for a pre-game skull session. He addressed himself mainly to Crossett, warning him against trying to split the vaunted Detroit defense of Reg Noble and Harvey "Rocky" Rockburn.

"These two guys have perfected the art of sandwiching attackers," said Smeaton. "Noble steers people into Rockburn and then Rockburn creams you. If you try to split them you can get hurt. And I mean hurt!"

Crossett appeared to be listening, but then in the second period Crossett stole the puck from a Detroit skater and did precisely what Smeaton had told him not to do. Archie Campbell, the Quakers' trainer, watched the play in awe from the Philadelphia bench.

"Noble got him first," Campbell remembers, "then Rockburn sent him flying off his feet. It was no ordinary hoist either. The big fellow seemed to take off like an airplane. Then he made a perfect three-point landing on elbows and stomach and started to skid along the ice. The wind had probably been knocked out of him before he ever touched the ice."

Many professional hockey players have mastered the art of the "swan dive," a maneuver designed to capture the referee's attention and obtain a penalty against the opposition. But everyone in the arena knew this time that Crossett was in trouble before he even landed.

"He was helpless," says Campbell. "He slid on his stomach from mid-ice right over to the boards with his stick extended in front of him. When the stick hit the boards, it jabbed Crossett's chin and knocked him out cold."

Unknown to Crossett, he had accidentally committed a foul on the play while he was in mid-air. It seems that his stick had snagged Rockburn, opening a bloody wound over Rocky's eye. While Crossett was stretched out unconscious on the ice he was given a five-minute major penalty by the referee for drawing blood!

Meanwhile, trainer Campbell dashed out on the ice to care for the injured Crossett. He waved smelling salts in front of the still Quaker until Stan came to his senses. Campbell then escorted him to the penalty box, helped place him on the bench, and then dangled more smelling salts until Crossett realized that he was neither in the dressing room nor on the Quakers' bench.

"What in Heaven's name am I doing *here*?" he asked of Campbell.

And calmly, as possible, Archie tried to explain.

It was Crossett who helped the Quakers as much as goalie Cude, who played spectacularly in the Philadelphia nets after his rather shaky start. Wilf's problem was that he was new to the NHL and consequently unfamiliar with the big guns on the opposition. Soon after he took over the goaltending job from Joe Miller, Cude went up against the mighty Montreal Maroons.

Coach Smeaton realized that his young goaler needed some special advice about the Montreal sharpshooters, particularly after Wilf's busy first period against the Maroons.

So between the first and second periods, Smeaton warned the Quakers to keep an eye on the "Big S" line of Nels Stewart, Hooley Smith, and Babe Siebert.

"Don't let that big lug Stewart stand too near our goal crease," warned Smeaton. "They don't call him 'Ole Poison' for nothing."

Edgy over the lecture, Cude broke in: "The hell with Stewart! I want my defense to keep an eye on that fellow wearing a cap. He's the one causing all my trouble."

The heretofore subdued Quakers' dressing room suddenly erupted with laughter; all except the befuddled Cude. Finally, coach Smeaton, wearing a big grin, leaned toward his netminder and whispered: "Wilfie, my boy, the chap with the cap *is* Nels Stewart."

Benny Leonard was quite willing to tolerate such shennanigans as long as his team put up a good fight; and that they did even though frequently undermanned.

On Christmas Day 1930, they pleased Benny no end while at the same time lost 8–0 to the Bruins at Boston Garden. The Quakers and Bruins indulged in a Pier Six free-for-all which began when Hib Milks was heavily checked by George Owen of Boston.

Nearly every player from both teams participated in the brawl with one notable exception—goalie Cude. This was as good a time as any for Wilfie to take a brief sabbatical from his trying job. And what Wilf saw from his vantage point in the crease was astonishing by any hockey-fight standards.

"Even the officials took a couple on the chin before it was over," wrote Charles L. Coleman in *The Trail of the Stanley Cup*. "As the referees seemed to be making very little headway in suppressing the fight, the police were called in. Only two constables went over the boards at first and they looked plaintively back for aid as they approached the melee. They were eventually joined by reinforcements."

After what seemed like hours of flailing sticks, crunching punches, and continuous bloodletting, the fighting eventually subsided. Referee Mickey Ion assessed major penalties with $15 fines to Owen, Eddie Shore, and Dit Clapper of the Bruins and to Milks, D'Arcy Coulson, and Allan Shields of Philadelphia.

From the Quakers' viewpoint, Clapper was the major culprit. He not only scored a three-goal hat trick against Cude but also knocked out Wally Kilrea of Philadelphia with a right cross to the chin.

A month later the Quakers showed their class, returning to Boston Garden for the first time since the 8–0 debacle. This time, goalie Cude looked like an Indian rubber man, contorting himself successfully well to help the Quakers to a 3–3 tie. It was such a remarkable performance that it even earned a line in the official NHL history. Cude followed that with a pair of wins over Detroit but it was too little, too late to save the Quakers.

The NHL Governors realized the depth of the Quakers' financial problems late in the season when the Montreal Canadiens decided to release defenseman Bert McCaffrey who surely would have helped the Philadelphia blue line corps. The waiver price was a mere $5000 and it was anticipated that Leonard would grab at the opportunity to bolster his team with an eye toward the next season. Instead, Leonard declined. Philadelphia had reached the bottom of the barrel.

Gallantly if not gloriously, the Quakers completed their

one and only season of NHL play on March 21, 1931, at the Forum in Montreal. Their opponents were the Canadiens, paced by Howie Morenz. Instead of lackadaisically playing out the string, the Quakers battled the Montrealers as if it were the final game for the Stanley Cup.

Matching the Canadiens goal for goal—the final score was 4–4—Philadelphia had the Forum crowd on *their* side, which stimulated the Montrealers to even more determined efforts. On one of his spectacular rushes down ice, Morenz dispatched a mighty shot at the Quakers' net. Cude lost sight of the rubber.

Before he could lift his glove to deflect the puck, it smashed against his jaw and sent him reeling backwards into the net while blood splattered across the goal crease. Cude was carried from the ice, suffering a torn jaw which required heavy stitching. Hugh McCormack, a former London, Ontario, goaltender-turned sportswriter, then put on the pads and preserved the 4–4 tie.

Rather than departing the NHL in a blaze of glory, the Quakers made their exit in a pool of red ink. On September 26, 1931, NHL president Frank Calder made it official that Philadelphia had agreed to suspend its franchise for one year.

Players belonging to the Quakers were distributed among the clubs which finished lowest in the league. One of them, left wing Syd Howe—no relation to Gordie Howe—was signed by Toronto and later dealt to Ottawa and St. Louis before landing in Detroit with the Red Wings. He was the only member of the Philadelphia sextet to gain permanent eminence. In June 1965 Howe was elected to the Hockey Hall of Fame. The others are just a vague memory to those who watched one of sport's most pathetic teams in action.

9/
Minor League but Mighty Good

The short, miserable life of Benny Leonard's Quakers did not spell the end of professional hockey in Philadelphia. If anything, the Quakers' demise proved to be a stimulus to the Arrows who not only continued operating but did something the Quakers never did—they began winning hockey games.

Herb Gardiner, who was originally signed to manage the Arrows in October 1929, emerged as a minor-league Mister Hockey in Philadelphia. He delivered a championship to the City of Brotherly Love in the 1932–33 season when the Arrows compiled a record of 29 victories, only 12 losses, and seven ties to finish in first place seven points ahead of runner-up Providence.

Unfortunately, the depression had hit the United States in the underbelly and many professional sports teams reeled from lack of attendance. There was talk of folding Philadelphia's sextet prior to the 1934–35 season because of losses at the gate. But on October 15, 1934, the club was saved when the Arrows receivers decided to run the team. Gardiner was retained as manager and members of the team which had been owned by Fitz-Eugene Dixon were to be lent to the Arrows.

This tenuous arrangement had its pitfalls—mostly on the ice where the Arrows fumbled and stumbled around, looking more like the defunct Quakers than anything else. Attendance at the Arena remained low and it was obvious that some transfusion of talent was necessary to save pro hockey in Philadelphia.

As Benny Leonard once predicted, the SOS sign was detected in New York City where Rangers manager, Lester Patrick decided he would kill—or save—two hockey teams with one shot. Patrick's theory was that a good big-league club was only as solid as its farm system and thus he became one of the first NHL leaders to develop a strong minor-league system, with each club's name bearing the initial letter R.

Thus, the Eastern Amateur Hockey League farm club was the Rovers. And when Patrick decided to swing a deal with the Arrows and pump life into them with new bodies, Philadelphia's team became known as the Ramblers. Patrick's plan received the blessing of Colonel John S. Hammond, chairman of the board of Madison Square Garden, who envisioned the Rangers operating the Philadelphia sextet for at least five years. The way the Colonel saw it, everybody would benefit.

"After the first year," said Hammond, sounding more and more like the ebullient Benny Leonard, "I can assure Philadelphia a championship team."

The difference between Leonard and Hammond is that the Colonel delivered. What's more he dispatched to Philadelphia some of the most gifted and colorful players ever to lace on skates. Many, such as Babe Pratt, Phil Watson, Bryan Hextall, and Joe Cooper, became legendary figures in the game.

When the 1935–36 edition of the Ramblers took the ice, they appeared powerful enough to take on some of the best clubs in the NHL. This pleased Patrick no end. Lester was particularly delighted with the Colville boys, Mac and Neil, who teamed up with Alex Shibicky to form a front line that he believed would some day be as good as the famed Cook Brothers—Bill and Bun—who together with Frank Boucher won two Stanley Cups for the Rangers.

Thanks to Watson, the Ramblers were as amusing as they were artistic. A native of Montreal, Watson grew up in a rather unique household. His father, a native of Glasgow, was a printer on a Montreal newspaper and spoke no French. His mother, a French-Canadian private nurse had mastered neither English nor any of the Scottish dialects.

The semantic set-tos in the Watson household were to have a lasting effect on Phillipe Henri's command of the English language, although his father had insisted that young Phil speak only English during his first six years.

However, shortly after his sixth birthday Phil got a job as an interpreter for a garbage-collector who covered an English-speaking district of Montreal and whose knowledge of the language was inadequate. It was an attractive position for a child of his years, since it paid a nickel a day, plus lunch.

Unfortunately for Phil, his mother returned home from work early one afternoon, learned of his employment, and, despite the strenuous objections of her husband, put him in a French private school 14 miles from Montreal. Young Phil remained in the school for ten years, at the end of which he had forgotten English entirely and could speak only French.

"After graduation," wrote Robert Lewis Taylor who was the biographer of another noted Philadelphian, W. C. Fields, "Watson returned to his family; renewing his acquaintance with his father by means of signs, he looked around for something to do. Mr. Watson, impressed by the athletic medals he had won at school, encouraged his son to take up a sport."

Since Phil preferred skating to bicycle-riding, billiards, or baseball, he decided to become a professional hockey player and eventually made his way to Philadelphia.

By the time Watson arrived on Broad Street his spoken English was audible but hardly understandable, and immediately he was singled out for all types of jokes.

A favorite pastime of the Colvilles was to read Watson's fan mail to him at those semi-formal gatherings attended by the entire squad. Watson would be seated in a chair, and one of the brothers, with a handful of spurious documents, over which he and the other Colville had labored at length, would take the floor facing him.

"Here's a number," Neil Colville once opened, "from a girl who signs herself Eloise Bockwurst."

Immediately, Watson's eyes lit up with joy and he chirped, "Good! Is nice. *Continuez.*"

"Dear Mr. Watson," Colville read, "in the many years I've been going to hockey games I've seen some cheesy performances, but nothing to compare with your exhibition of last Tuesday. You skate like you were carrying a walrus on your back. You're so ugly, too. I'm . . ."

By this time Watson was in high dudgeon. "I keel all these damn *Américains*," he cried. "I queet. I go home!"

When Watson wasn't carrying on in the Philadelphia dressing room, Walter "Babe" Pratt could be counted on for some form of raillery. Once Pratt was playing in a game being refereed by an official well-fortified with brandy. Whenever there was a faceoff in Babe's defensive zone, he would take the draw; and whenever Pratt prepared to take the draw the referee leaned over Babe's shoulder to drop the puck.

"Sir," said Pratt politely to the referee. "Would you mind leaning over my opponent's shoulder when you drop the puck? You're making *me* drunk."

Another time, Pratt was asked to describe his team. "This is a great team," boasted Babe. "We have an unbeatable combination: hungry rookies and thirsty veterans."

Under Herb Gardiner's able management, the Ramblers blossomed. "Gardiner developed in that season," said Tom Lockhart, former New York Rangers' business manager, "what was probably the greatest team Philadelphia has ever had on ice."

The team finished in first place with 27 victories, 18 losses, and three ties, nine points ahead of runner-up Providence. The Ramblers then whipped Providence in the best-of-five playoff finals, three games to one. It was enough to catapult Watson and Pratt into the NHL in the 1936–37 season, but Philadelphia remained stronger than ever.

Clint Smith and Bryan Hextall took over where Watson had left off in what now became the International-American League, a seven-team, two-division offshoot of the Can-Am and International Leagues. Philadelphia was spotted in the Eastern Division along with Springfield, Providence, and

New Haven. Syracuse, Pittsburgh, and Cleveland comprised the Western Division.

As expected, the Quakers captured the Eastern title with a record of 26 wins, 14 losses, and eight ties for 60 points. While in the West, Syracuse was the victor with 27 victories, 16 losses, and five ties for 59 points. Philadelphia had the top point mark in the league.

In the playoffs, however, after dropping the opening game to the Quakers, 2–0, Syracuse won three in a row to capture the series. Nobody knew it at the time, but the golden era of minor-league hockey in Philadelphia was coming to an end.

Delighted with the maturing of his farmhands, Lester Patrick elevated Hextall, Smith, the Colvilles, and Shibicky to the Rangers who were to win a Stanley Cup in 1940 with these former Ramblers comprising the nucleus of the club. The Ramblers slipped to second in 1937–38, climbed back to first in the Eastern Division a year later, and then dropped to last in 1939–40.

What once was a flood of young talent moving up to the parent Rangers had become a trickle by 1940 when left wing Herb Foster of the Quakers finished in a tie for Rookie of the Year honors with Hank Goldup of the Pittsburgh Hornets.

"I watched Herb play for seven years," said Redvers Mackenzie, a well-respected minor league hockey coach, "and in all that time I never saw anyone check him effectively, even in a single game."

Ken Murray, a splendid minor-leaguer, had been assigned to cover Foster several times and marvelled at his finesse. "Foster," Murray observed, "is the only player I cannot handle at least fairly well. I always think I have him covered until I see the puck in the net."

But Foster remained nothing more than "a good minor-leaguer," played only five games with the Rangers, and spent the remainder of his career down on the farm. By the 1940–41 season World War II had taken a large number of Canadian-born hockey players into the armed forces. The Quakers, despite Foster's glittering play, finished last in the Eastern Division (25–25–6) and, of course, out of the playoffs. Shortly thereafter the Rangers announced that they were moving their farm out of Philadelphia.

As soon as the Rangers' exit was made public, a group of Philadelphians quickly seized the occasion and took over the American League franchise. They renamed their "new" club THE ROCKETS, because, as one Philadelphia newspaper rather condescendingly observed: "Arena officials feel fans will quickly become familiar with the new name because it begins with an 'R' and is similar to Ramblers, the name of the team the Rockets displace."

Right from the start, the Rockets were in trouble. Big trouble. Canada's new wartime regulations made it difficult for men of military age to cross the border into the United States to play hockey. But, somehow, new coach Danny Cox managed to put together a patchwork squad that had more fight than finesse. Among the more rambunctious members of the squad were defenseman Bill Moe, who later was to perfect the submarine hip check, Harry Dick who would fight any one any time, and Vic Lofvendahl, who had been imported from the Pacific Coast League.

They fought well but the best-remembered fighter of all was Rocket forward Ossie Asmundsen, who battled Vic Myles of the New Haven Eagles on the night of December 6, 1941—Pearl Harbor Eve—at the Philadelphia Arena.

"Men who had been watching hockey for years," commented writer Earl Eby, "say it was the worst they had ever witnessed."

The fight erupted late in the third period when Myles cracked the Philadelphia skater over the head with his stick. Asmundsen counterattacked but officials quickly intervened and gave each player a two-minute roughing penalty.

"As they were about to enter the penalty box," wrote Eby, "Myles hit Asmundsen in the mouth with his bare fist. And as quick as a rattlesnake strikes, Asmundsen brought his stick down on Myles' head. Then the two men came together. They landed on the ice, and both of them, well-versed in the art, began bringing up the sharp blades of their skates. Asmundsen once succeeded in sinking the ends of his blades in Myles' back."

By now the bloodbath had become so bitter that Rocket goalie Alfie Moore motioned for the police to intervene before one of the gladiators was killed.

"Three policemen stood in the penalty box after being summoned by Moore," said Eby, "but they looked on hardly believing their eyes. After a few minutes the two battlers were so exhausted they fell apart and it was then they were separated. The ice in front of the penalty box was crimson."

After being examined by doctors on the scene, Myles emerged from the infirmary with five stitches in his scalp; while Asmundsen suffered loosened teeth, a bruised nose, and scratched face. The Rockets won the hockey game, 3–1.

Philadelphia salvaged only 10 other games in that 56 game schedule to finish a poor last in their division. Considering the manpower shortage, the Rockets were fortunate to end the season with a full complement of players; and now that the United States had entered the war, things would become even more difficult for the American League teams.

By September 1942, when Rocket officials began planning for the new season, not only were players impossible to find but their coach Danny Cox was confined to his home city of Port Arthur, Ontario, where he was engaged in war work.

On September 15, 1942, the Rockets, like Benny Leonard's Quakers, folded after one season of play. "We thought of operating another Rockets' team," said manager Pete Tyrrell, "but when we tried to get in touch with our players we discovered that only five of them would be available. It was a blow to us to have finished in last place last season and we didn't want to struggle through with another cellar club. This city deserves better representation."

But no matter how desperate the manpower shortage, Philadelphia was destined to have an organized hockey team in the 1942–43 season and, almost miraculously, it did—in the Eastern Amateur Hockey League.

The EAHL was a curious organization masterminded by Tom Lockhart, who also doubled as an executive for the Rangers. The league was a member of the United States Amateur Hockey Association which had been organized on October 29, 1937, by Lockhart and several associates. Needless to say, Lockhart was its president and remained top banana for more than three decades.

What made the EAHL so unusual was that despite their amateur label—according to definition, an amateur is any player who does not sign a professional contract—the EAHL players were paid regular salaries, competed in a 46 game schedule, not including playoffs, and were regarded as pros by everyone except those who found it convenient to call them amateurs.

The Rangers thought so highly of the EAHL as a breeding ground for talent that they placed a team, the Rovers, in there as did other NHL clubs. The result was a flourishing organization, featuring first-rate hockey at low prices. World War II, however, put a crimp in the Eastern League's operation; and by the start of the 1942–43 campaign, it appeared that Lockhart's circuit might have to shut down.

But the effervescent Irishman would have none of it. When the Baltimore Orioles—EAHL champions in 1940—were forced to fold, Lockhart realized that several professional hockey stars who had enlisted in the United States Coast Guard were stationed nearby.

So a Coast Guard team was organized and admitted to the EAHL for the 1942–43 season. Thanks to the Rangers, the Rovers remained alive and the Boston Bruins sponsored an Eastern League team too: the Olympics. One more team was needed to round out the EAHL for 1942–43 season and Lockhart managed to place one in Philadelphia's Arena.

This was a patchwork sextet comprised of homebrews, such as goalie Barney Geisel, and the slick: youngsters Marty Madore and Tommy Brennan. Like the Rockets whom they succeeded, the Falcons made up in fight what they lacked in finesse. Though unfortunately for them the Eastern League was bulging with battlers in that wartime year.

Most of the fighters were sprinkled down the long Coast Guard Cutters roster, whose Curtis Bay team was filled with such big-leaguers as New York Ranger captain Art Coulter; Johnny Mariucci, the "badman" of the Chicago Black Hawks; and Frankie Brimsek, Mister Zero of the Boston Bruins.

In addition to the NHL aces who had enlisted in the Coast Guard, the Cutters also boasted several first-rate minor professionals including Manny Cotlow, an awesome Jewish defenseman who had played in the American Association.

One night in February 1943, Cotlow led the Cutters—also known as "Hooligan's Navy"—into Philadelphia's Arena and single-handedly started his own private war.

Cotlow, who wore his black hair slicked down on both sides of a center part like actor George Raft, started the ruckus by taking on Marty Madore of the Falcons late in the second period. Although calmed by the officials, Cotlow and Madore went at it again when they reached the penalty box which, unlike today's separate benches, was a communal seat.

Enraged by Cotlow, several Philadelphia rooters attacked the huge Coast Guard defenseman. "They leaned over the rails," said Philadelphia hockey writer Stan Baumgartner, "and began to swing fists—some of which landed on Cotlow's chin and cheek. Coast Guard players rushed to Cotlow's aid. Bob Dill and Art Coulter climbed to the concrete walk circling the ice and began using their sticks as a gunman would use a blackjack.

"The pointed end of their sticks flattened the soft hats of two would-be Dempseys. Police rushed to the scene. Everyone started swinging. The penalty box looked like a sardine can. Another battle started on the ice with the referee and linesman soon on their knees in a hand-to-hand struggle with the players of both teams. The police finally got control and the spectators were shooed back to their seats."

The Cutters, who rarely lost to anybody, won the game, 9–4.

Considering their personnel problems, the Falcons provided Arena spectators with an entertaining brand of hockey in 1942–43, although they finished last (fourth) with a record of 17 wins, 27 losses, and two ties.

Now that they had a full season under their belts Phil Thompson, owner of the Falcons, and coach Red Mackenzie expected bigger things in 1943–44. This time they had enough breathing room to search the continent for players and by November 6, 1943, when they opened at the Arena against the Boston Olympics, Philadelphia had a competent, if not championship, team.

The brothers Orville and Clayton Lavell and Squee Allen were among the better forwards while their defense was anchored by one of the most threatening backliners in major or minor league hockey, Joe Desson. A quiet, bespectacled gentleman off ice, Desson was apt to go haywire at any time during a game; and frequently without warning.

And Heaven help the referee who happened to cross Desson's path at the wrong time. Early in the 1944–45 season Desson did flatten one official and was suspended for two weeks by EAHL President Lockhart. Though, as always, Joe was the acme of penitence after his explosion.

"All I want is another chance," said Desson. "I will try to mend my ways. I want it understood, however, that I never deliberately tried to injure another player. That's why I fought instead of using my stick."

When Desson wasn't fighting he was as good as any defenseman in the league. However, the Falcons' problem at the start of the 1943–44 campaign was elsewhere. Nick Pidsodny, who started the season in the nets for Philadelphia and who later would star for the Baltimore Blades, disappointed coach Mackenzie who went searching for another goaltender. His choice was a little fellow from North Battleford, Saskatchewan: Emile "The Cat" Francis.

Francis, who'd had a tryout with the Detroit Red Wings earlier in the season, went up against the EAHL powerhouse, the Boston Olympics. The Cat lost, 3–0, but he won the press notices. "He played a great game," wrote Earl Eby. "Shots that escaped him can be excused. He's a baby-faced kid who hasn't seen much action in the company he was in last night. But the boy is a comer. Fans gave him a great hand. . . . There's hope for the Falcons."

Francis was as happy about playing in Philadelphia as the Philadelphians were delighted to have him on their side. Decades later, as general manager–coach of the Rangers, Francis reminisced about his Eastern League stint with the Falcons.

"The thing I remember most," he said, "was my first trip to New York with the Falcons. We took the train into Penn Station and then Red Mackenzie hustled out off the platform. I thought we were going first-class and would take cabs to Madison Square Garden.

"Instead, Mackenzie said, 'Alright, you guys, everybody into the subway.' We wound up taking the subway two stops to 50th Street where the old Garden used to be. That was probably the only time in my life I regretted being a goalkeeper. It was murder riding the New York subway with the huge goal bag on my shoulder."

Mackenzie brooked no tomfoolery from his players and anyone who considered challenging his authority first had to consider the sign on the dressing room door in Philadelphia: "TRAINS LEAVING FOR CANADA EVERY HOUR ON THE HOUR."

Francis and Mackenzie got along better than Francis and

the ancient Philadelphia Arena, with its assorted and sordid built-in obstacles.

"The Arena," said Francis, "was a very dangerous place for a player. For starters, you had to step down into that hole and the boards were only three feet high, at the most, and up above that there were railings. It's a miracle nobody got killed with that kind of arrangement.

"If you rolled a guy up against the boards, the boards were so low the guy would wind up cracking against the steel fence. And that really could hurt a man."

As a member of the Falcons, Francis was paid $50 a week; but because of a curious Canadian-American monetary agreement, the young goalie only got half that amount. "I received $25," he recalls, "and the other $25 was deposited in my account in Canada. So I actually had to manage on $25 a week."

Francis only played one season for the Falcons. A year later he tended goal for the Washington Lions of the Eastern League. Meanwhile, the Falcons continued to play sparkling, if not championship, hockey. The closest they came to winning an Eastern League pennant was in the 1945–46 season. They then tied the Boston Olympics in the playoffs but lost the right to play in the national championship on the Pacific Coast because Boston had scored more goals.

Unquestionably, the Falcons had sold hockey in Philadelphia. What remained to be seen was whether Philadelphians would once again see big-league hockey, a first-rate minor league brand, or remain with the EAHL variety.

The answer would be forthcoming in the Spring of 1946.

10/

And Then There Were None

As the 1945–46 hockey season reached the homestretch, a relatively unfamiliar word was introduced at the NHL Governors' meeting in New York's Hotel Commodore. Expansion.

Applications accompanied by certified checks for $10,000 were received from Los Angeles, San Francisco, and Philadelphia. The bidder for Philadelphia was Len Peto, who had an option on the old Montreal Maroons' franchise.

Peto was said to command $2,500,000 with which to build a new Philadelphia arena and ice a major league team. Enthusiastic as they may have appeared at first, the NHL governors eventually shunted the bids aside and Peto's plan went down the drain.

Undaunted, Philadelphians continued to clamor for professional hockey once more and on June 13, 1946, Pete Tyrrell, general manager of the Arena announced that Philadelphia would move up the ladder from the EAHL back to the American League. The name reverted to the Rockets and Herb Gardiner once again took command.

Little good can be said about the return to the AHL, except that Gardiner obtained right wing Phil Hergesheimer, a gifted forward who led the league in scoring while also coaching the club.

But Hergesheimer couldn't do it alone and the Rockets plumbed the depths of the AHL. It was then felt if Hergesheimer was relieved of coaching chores, he might score even more goals and the Rockets would climb higher during the 1947–48 season.

With that in mind, Hergesheimer was replaced as coach by Wally Kilrea who previously had coached at Fort Worth in the United States League. Ironically, the Rockets did play better under the new arrangement but Hergesheimer dropped way down the scoring list.

Neither Hergesheimer nor a record-breaking defenseman named Eddie Bush could rescue the Rockets. A series of losing seasons following on the heels of the moderately successful Falcons virtually doomed the team and in January 1949 Tyrrell hinted that his club might fold unless it could find a major league affiliate. He also explained that the limited seating capacity of the Arena made it difficult for an AHL team to turn a profit.

Two months later the Rockets died, only this time two years elapsed before the Eastern League Falcons returned to the scene.

It was hoped that Eastern League hockey would prove as appealing to Philadelphians as it had in the mid-Forties but this was not to be the case and just before Christmas 1951 the Falcons folded for good. "The attendance," said Tyrrell, "has proven that there are not enough Philadelphians interested in hockey to warrant continuing."

Tyrrell was only half right. Philadelphians, it would later be shown, certainly could be attracted to hockey if the game was presented in an appealing enough package. And that is precisely what happened in October 1955 when the Ramblers were revived as an Eastern League franchise.

With veteran Eastern Leaguer Edgar "Chirp" Brenchley behind the bench, the Ramblers immediately signed a first-rate goaler named Ivan Walmsley. "I predict," announced Brenchley, "that Ivan will be the best goaltender in the Eastern League."

Brenchley did not make an idle boast; Walmsley was not just good, he was superior and at the end of the 1956–57 season was named the league's most valuable player. This came after a noble effort the year before when the Ramblers were just barely nosed out of a playoff berth on a questionable referee's decision.

Despite the non-playoff season, both spectators and journalistic critics were pleased with the entertainment. "The Ramblers," wrote John Brogan of *The Bulletin*, "were a very funny team. They did funny things and were even funny to look at. They boasted a Mutt and Jeff combination named Ray Crew and Rocky Rukavina. Neither could play hockey well but both were excellent entertainers. Crew was 6'4" and weighed 220 pounds. Rukavina was 5'4", 145. As could be expected, Crew was forever menacing the opponents' little men while Rocky spent most of his time on the ice scrapping with the big boys. The fans loved it."

They loved it even more in 1956–57 because the Ramblers were not only funny, they were good; so good that they went all the way to the playoff finals before being defeated by the Charlotte Clippers. It seemed another golden era might be in store for the Eastern League sextet, except that the front office was being run on a shoestring and the owners were thinking small instead of big-time.

Defenseman Crew, who was the most popular Rambler, one–two with Rukavina, was released after a dispute over a $10 raise with the club owners. Then, there was the Bill Kurtz incident. A member of the Ramblers' first line, Kurtz was among the team's leading scorers yet he was released by the club on the grounds that he "wasn't good enough to play with them anymore."

Not surprisingly, Kurtz packed away his skates for life after that development. "A team that operated like this," said Brogan who eventually became a public relations executive with the Flyers, "couldn't succeed for long." And the Ramblers didn't.

In the Spring of 1960 George L. Davis, Jr., president of the club, declared voluntary bankruptcy for the Ramblers. Two months later Ambrose "Bud" Dudley, former athletic director at Villanova University, stepped in and organized a syndicate to run the franchise.

Anticipating the women's liberation movement by some years, Dudley named Connie Williams as the Ramblers' assistant general manager. She became the first woman to run an Eastern League team and she promptly went to work signing new faces.

Ms. Williams divined the Indians' rights movement and signed Harley Hodgson, a full-blooded Indian to a Ramblers' contract. The movement suffered a stunning blow, however, when it was discovered that Harley could hardly skate.

Other acquisitions fared better. John Brophy, a gray-haired defenseman who resembled a foreign service diplomat, surpassed Ray Crew's popularity as a battling defenseman. Unlike the big, galumphing Crew, Brophy was a dexterous skater whose only problem was that he had the lowest boiling point in organized hockey.

Once, he engaged Russ McClenaghan in a vicious stick fight and was cut about the head. In the trainer's room for repairs and still sizzling with anger, Brophy became impatient with the doctor who was delicately but too slowly stitching his wound. Suddenly, Brophy bolted from the trainer's table and dashed for the door while the doctor tried to keep up with him, fingering the needle and thread which remained attached to Brophy's gray head.

Surely, Brophy would be suspended for his intemperance, especially since Eastern League president Tom Lockhart was known to be attending the game that night. A few minutes later a reporter spotted Lockhart and asked what manner of penalty he'd inflict on Brophy.

"I don't know yet," said Lockhart, "I didn't see the fight."

"How could you miss it?" the other asked. "It lasted for ten minutes."

"Oh," Lockhart laconically replied, "I was in the office having a drink."

The Philadelphia tradition for tough hockey players was continued by Bob Bailey, a former Toronto Maple Leafs forward who would think nothing of clobbering a goaltender.

Bailey did this one night to Marv Edwards, who later advanced to the NHL. The deftness of Bailey's execution was such that only Bailey, himself, knew why Edwards was stretched horizontal on the ice for nearly half a minute after the Rambler forward had applied an elbow.

At the end of the game reporters questioned Bailey about

the episode. Why would he clobber an innocent goalie? "Simple," Bailey replied, "he talks too much."

It was an ironic remark since Bailey never stopped talking during his tenure in Philadelphia. He eventually became player–coach and remained in that position for a full seven games before he talked himself right off the team. The vehicle for Bailey's departure was the Ramblers' own team bus, which was used for road trips and, according to seasoned bus-watchers, was smaller than most. Bailey didn't think it was fit for pigs much less hockey players and told the Ramblers' management so.

"It's nothing but a truck with some seats in it," Bailey complained. "I told them to get rid of it, but they wouldn't. That's when I resigned.

"The bus is bad for the morale of the team. It's uncomfortable and poses a hardship on the players. And they had the nerve to paint PHILADELPHIA RAMBLERS HOCKEY CLUB across the side. We're the laughingstock of the league.

"The bus broke down twice on our Southern trip," Bailey added. "Once, outside of Charlotte, we all had to get out and push it down the highway. The people thought the circus had arrived."

Bailey's stand impressed Leonard Tose, the Ramblers' majority stockholder. He told Bailey that he had dealt with truckdrivers and unions but that Bob was the toughest man he had ever handled. Bailey thanked him but pointed out he merely wanted to have a winning hockey team and claimed that was impossible with the Ramblers' Toonerville bus.

"Funny thing," said Bailey, "but a couple of days after we got home, somebody threw a brick through the windshield. It might have looked as if I did it, but I didn't."

What Bailey did do was quit the team and take four players with him. By the end of the season the major stockholders were battling among themselves and, once again, the city's hockey franchise was teetering on the brink of oblivion. In August 1964 Pete Tyrrell, operator of the Arena, tried to keep it alive by applying for a new Eastern League franchise but the league refused the application and, instead, granted one to a New Jersey group, operating a team out of the Cherry Hill Arena in suburban Haddonfield, New Jersey. Bud Dudley, erstwhile president of the Ramblers, was named a co-director of the new club.

Philadelphia hockey fans were considerably upset. Lou Damia, president of the Rambler Rooters Club, dispatched a letter of protest to Eastern League president Lockhart and suggested his group might boycott the games in nearby Cherry Hill.

"When Dudley and his players crossed the river," wrote *Philadelphia Daily News* sports editor Ben Callaway, "they may have left many of their old athletic supporters behind."

Perhaps, but the demise of the Ramblers was to pave the way for a return of major league hockey.

It was evident that fresh money and a new arena would be necessary. A four-man group headed by William Putnam and including Philadelphia Eagles' president Jerry Wolman had the money and the blueprints for a new arena. On February 8, 1966, they formally applied for a franchise in the NHL.

In one day the NHL Governors, meeting at the St. Regis Hotel near Central Park in Manhattan, would decide whether Philadelphia would be one of the six new expansion teams. Putnam was skeptical. Moments before the owners made their decision, he paced the floor in his suite at the nearby Plaza Hotel.

"Just about ten minutes from now," said Putnam, "that phone will ring and I'll be out of business again."

Less than a minute later the phone rang. The voice on the other end belonged to Bill Jennings, president of the New York Rangers and architect of NHL expansion. "Bill," said Jennings, "you're in!"

Philadelphia was back in hockey's big tent; only this time to stay.

The Whittington sisters—Frances, Julia, and Helen (left to right), who rank among Philadelphia's original hockey fans, display their ancient Arrow programs as well as photos of favorites Joe Desson and Bill Moe. March 1946.—*UPI*

Usually the object of official wrath, Falcon's captain Joe Desson receives the Hershey Trophy from President Tom Lockhart in March 1946 after the Falcons finished second in the Eastern League.

—*Wide World*

The start of one of hockey's most vicious stick fights between Boston's Eddie Shack (left) and the Flyers' Larry Zeidel at Maple Leaf Gardens. (The Spectrum had been temporarily closed.) March 7, 1968.

—*Canadian Press*

Ouch! St. Louis Blues center Red Berenson backhands the puck over goalie Doug Favell at the Spectrum on November 7, 1968, the night Red scored a record-tying six goals in one game. Final score: St. Louis 8, Flyers 0. *Ouch* again!—*UPI*

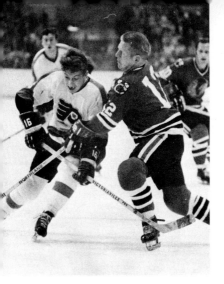

A youthful Bobby Clarke tries the overland route past Chicago's Pat Stapleton in 1969.—*UPI*

Right: Clarke (16) changes direction at the blue line in pursuit of you-know-what.—*UPI*

He scores! Jean-Guy Gendron beats St. Louis goalie Ernie Wakely while Bob Plager does the old soft shoe. Circa 1970.—*UPI*

On the theory that "if you can't beat 'em, join 'em," Bobby Clarke joins the melee in front of the Bruins' goal while Bobby Orr moves in from the left.
—*UPI*

Gary Dornhoefer does the Charleston with Jerry Korab.—*UPI*

Right: Ed Van Impe (left) does what he does best: deposits the enemy from vertical to horizontal; in this case, Bill Fairbairn of the Rangers.—*UPI*

Serge Bernier in a nest of Black Hawks. November 1971.—*UPI*

Nobody, it seems, likes the Blues in Philadelphia, including the Spectrum guards who here exchange pleasantries with St. Louis defenseman—orator Bob Plager in January 1972.—*UPI*

Bob Kelly (center) and Bobby Clarke (right) take sides against Minnesota goalie Gump Worsley.—*UPI*

The bearded wonder, Bill
Flett.—*Joel Bernbaum*

Clarke, playing Mercury,
overtakes the Flying
Frenchmen.
                 —*Joel Bernbaum*

Left: Bong! The Three Stooges couldn't have done it better. Ross Lonsberry bops Craig Patrick of the California Seals. November 1972.—*UPI*

Right: Van Impe (right) attempts to slow down New York's Ted Irvine.
—*Frank Bryan*

Clarke (right) and Toronto's Jim McKenny mix it up a bit.—*UPI*

Goalie Wayne Stephenson of St. Louis is down and Gary Dornhoefer is up. The puck, of course, is in.—*UPI*

Mismatch? Maybe. Anyway it took three Canadiens to box Clarke out for the moment.—*UPI*

Before suffering a heart attack, Flyers' goalie Bruce Gamble starred against Montreal, here stopping Rejean Houle.—*UPI*

Double lightning on ice, Gene Carr of the Rangers and Bobby Clarke.—*UPI*

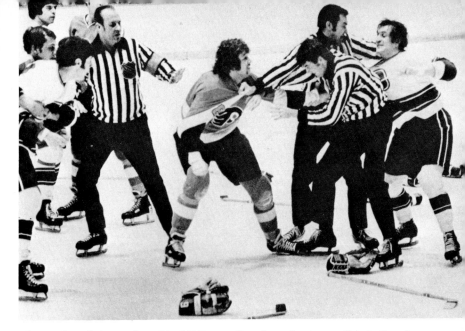

The night of December 29, 1972, produced a classic confrontation in Vancouver between the fans, the players, and the police. Here Dave Schultz of the Flyers and Bobby Schmautz of the Canucks attempt to outflank the linesmen.—*UPI*

A few nights later in Atlanta, things were much the same.—*UPI*

Wayne Hillman attempts to embed Dan Maloney along the sideboards.—*UPI*

Right: Doug Favell foils Frank Mahovlich (center) and Henri Richard (left). —*Joel Bernbaum*

Canadian-American relations occasionally become strained when the Flyers and Canadiens get together for an evening of play.—*UPI*

Close but no goal, as the Islanders' Bill Smith snares the rubber away from Dave Schultz.—*UPI*

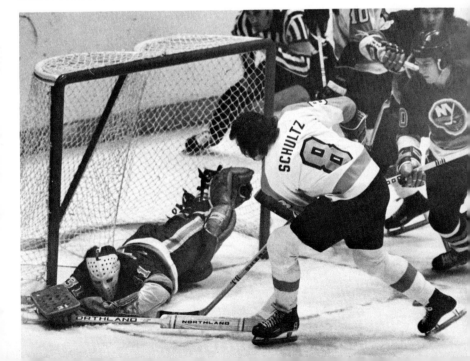

Favell in motion.—*Joel Bernbaum*

MVP Bobby Clarke muscles past Montreal defensemen Guy Lapointe (5) and Larry Robinson to beat goalie Michel Plasse in February 1973 at the Forum.—*UPI*

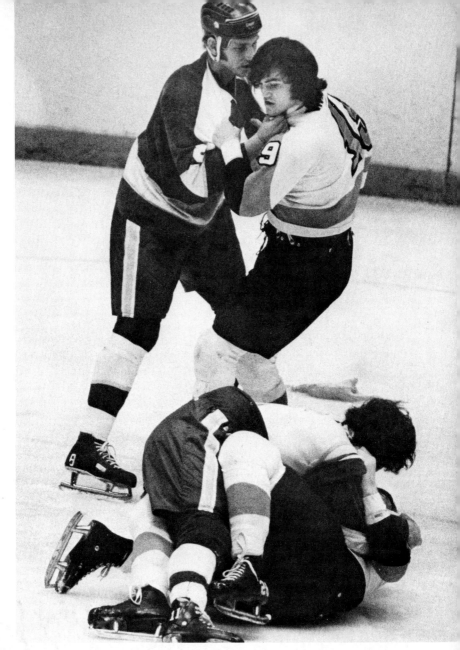

Do I hear a waltz? Bill Goldsworthy of Minnesota (left) and Rick Mac-Leish dance around Danny Grant of the North Stars as he rocks atop Don Saleski of the Flyers.—*UPI*

The biggest goal of 1972–73. Rick MacLeish's shot flashes past Montreal's Ken Dryden at 2:56 of the first overtime period in the first game of the Stanley Cup semi-final round at the Forum.—*UPI*

And Rick then does a jig to celebrate.—*UPI*

I'll drink to that. Coach Fred Shero prepares a toast for Bobby Clarke after the Flyers' captain won the Hart Trophy in May 1973.—*UPI*

11 /

A New NHL Team Is Born

The idea of expanding the NHL from its tightly knit six-team cocoon to a more ambitious eight- or twelve-team organization had been bruited about by its governors for years.

In one corner were members of the Old Guard, led by Big Jim Norris, president of the Chicago Black Hawks who found the cozy, six-team league entirely to his liking. Representatives of the Toronto Maple Leafs and Montreal Canadiens were inclined to go along with this view and it held fast as long as the balance of power remained on the northern side of the United States–Canadian border.

But the balance began shifting in the early Sixties when Toronto and Montreal patriarchs, Conn Smythe and Frank Selke, Sr., respectively, left their hockey posts for lives in semi-retirement. The power vacuum had to be filled, which is precisely when William "Bill" Jennings, a grey-haired Manhattan attorney entered the picture.

Following a shuffle of Madison Square Garden officials, Jennings had become president of the New York Rangers and, after a year or so feeling his way around the NHL, began to establish himself as a quiet but very aggressive young governor. Jennings favored expansion of the NHL's horizons as much as the Old Guard opposed it. Except that the Old Guard had dwindled and the harder Jennings pushed, the more ground he gained.

At first, Jennings' other prime opponent was NHL President Clarence Campbell who had been in office since 1946 and enjoyed the status quo as much as any conservative. "There's no point in expanding," Campbell would argue, "because we're doing very well now, filling our rinks to almost 98 percent of capacity."

Which was exactly Jennings' point. The Rangers' president theorized that if six teams could make a lot of money filling their rinks every night for 70 games, twelve teams could do likewise. And, besides, the six new teams would ante up something like $2,000,000 apiece which would make the original six even richer.

By 1965 Jennings had won his point and a series of quiet maneuvers had begun within the NHL hierarchy to establish a clear blueprint for expansion from six to twelve teams. The target date was 1967–68. Feelers were dispatched through the sports-investors grapevine that six big-league hockey franchises would be available and, almost immediately, the responses began filtering in to Campbell's office.

One of them was from Philadelphia.

Bill Putnam, handsome vice president of Morgan Guaranty Trust Company, signed the letter to Campbell. Putnam previously had made sports news in Philadelphia by helping Jerry Wolman finance the Philadelphia Eagles football team.

The Eagles hierarchy included Ed Snider, who had made a fortune in the record business, and his brother-in-law Earl

Foreman. After getting his feet wet in the Eagles' enterprise, Snider had the sports bug; and so when Putnam's letter went to Campbell, Snider appeared as an "associate" along with builder Jerry Schiff, Snider's other brother-in-law.

Eventually, Snider emerged with 60 percent of the Flyers while beer baron Joe Scott obtained 15 percent when Schiff made his exit. Putnam's 25 percent was bought up in time by F. Eugene Dixon, Jr.

The Philadelphia application was accepted by the NHL along with Oakland, Los Angeles, St. Louis, Pittsburgh, and Minnesota. At least one respected syndicated columnist predicted that the Flyers would last about as long as the Philadelphia Quakers. Putnam bridled at the forecast and went about the business of setting up a first-rate hockey organization. His immediate needs were for a general manager to find the right players and sign them and for a coach to guide this collection into the West Division playoffs.

Sensitive to critics, Putnam was quick to assure Philadelphians that big-league hockey the second time around would be better than Benny Leonard's production of 1930. "We have better credentials," said Putnam. "Our new rink, the Spectrum, will be the best hockey arena ever built."

Ground was broken for the Spectrum on June 1, 1966. The $12,000,000 brick and glass oval building on Broad Street and Pattison Avenue was completed 15 months later. The men assigned to deliver a winner to the building were general manager Norman "Bud" Poile and coach Keith Allen.

Prior to joining the Flyers, Poile's teams had missed making the playoffs only twice in 16 years. A veteran NHL forward, he had played with five of the six established big-league clubs and was renowned for his powerful shot. Poile had been a principal in one of hockey's biggest trades when he was dispatched to Chicago from Toronto along with Gus Bodnar, Gaye Stewart, Ernie Dickens, and Bob Goldham for Max Bentley during the 1947–48 season.

Allen was Poile's choice as coach. Although he had seen limited action in the NHL, Allen was respected as a solid minor-league defenseman and had become one of the more popular coaches after he quit playing.

Poile and Allen then picked Marcel Pelletier, a gregarious former goaltender, as their trouble-shooter, and Alec Davidson, previously with the Toronto Maple Leafs organization, as chief scout.

The front office quartet were put to their first major test on June 6, 1967, when they attended the NHL draft to select 20 players for the new team.

Managers from each of the six new teams drew lots to form an order of selection and Poile came out second. The category was goaltenders and he had an appetizing choice, headed by Glenn "Mister Goalie" Hall formerly with the Chicago Black Hawks, Charlie Hodge of the Montreal Canadiens, who had helped win the Vezina Trophy as well as a few Stanley Cups, and the efficient Don Simmons.

Poile stunned the crowd by bypassing all of those veterans and selecting 22-year-old French-Canadian Bernie Parent of the Boston Bruins. On his second time around, Poile again ignored Simmons and, this time, plucked Doug Favell, another Bruins' chattel who is two days younger than Parent. It was a deft decision and precisely what the Flyers front office had wanted.

"Parent and Favell have been teammates on championship

clubs in amateur and minor league hockey," said Allen. "They complement each other well. After the Bruins protected Gerry Cheevers, we could have taken Eddie Johnston, who has more NHL experience, but he's 31 and we think Parent is a better prospect."

Time would prove Allen right. Now that they were well-fortified in goal, the Flyers went about the business of stocking the other positions. To their amazement, the Chicago Black Hawks had left their crack defenseman Ed Van Impe unprotected and he was immediately claimed by Poile. Another ex-Chicago defender John Miszuk was picked along with ex-Bruins Joe Watson and Dick Cherry. From the Montreal Canadiens, the Flyers obtained husky backliner Jean Gauthier who for the time being rounded out their blue line corps.

In the third round of the draft Poile began concentrating on forwards. He landed Brit Selby who, two years earlier, had been NHL Rookie of the Year at Toronto and Lou Angotti, a smallish but fleet center who had been a Black Hawk and would be the Flyers team captain that first year. One of his most important choices had to wait for the 12th round when Gary Dornhoefer was plucked from the Bruins.

Other forward choices included Leon Rochefort from Montreal, Don Blackburn from Toronto, Forbes Kennedy from Boston, Pat Hannigan from Chicago, Dwight Carruthers from Detroit, Bob Courcy from Montreal, and Keith Wright from Boston.

It was an era without sports attorneys and Poile promptly went about the business of signing his choices. To get Parent, he motored to Haliburton, Ontario (population 853) by the shores of Lake Kashagawigamog where young Bernie was teaching at a hockey school. Poile signed him to a three-year contract at an estimated $20,000 per season.

"We offered Parent a three-year contract," said Poile, "to show we have confidence in him. He's young, has a great future, and we don't want him worrying about his contract."

One by one the Flyers put pen to the dotted line and by October 6, 1967, Philadelphia had a 19-man roster that was ready to begin the 1967–68 campaign.

Experts believed that it would be competitive within the West Division but not of championship caliber. The favorites were the Oakland Seals whose lineup was sprinkled with first-rate NHL skaters and veteran goalie Hodge.

"We've got to be in the top three in the expansion division," said Poile, following an exhibition record of three wins, three losses, and two ties. "I think we're going to jell and be a factor in the race."

Goaltending was the Flyers' strong suit and it was difficult to choose between the brooding Parent and the effervescent Favell. "Right now," commented coach Allen a week before opening night, "I'd guess that Favell will be our starter."

As in every training camp, there were surprises. For the Flyers it was 29-year-old center Ed Hoekstra, a minor-league veteran who won a job on the big team. "I never thought he had a chance to make the club," Poile conceded. "Never considered him. But his line with Bill Sutherland and Leon Rochefort has been our best."

The Flyers opened the season on October 11, 1967, at Oakland, losing 5–1 to the Seals. On October 14, they lost, 4–2, to the Los Angeles Kings. Their first victory came in the third game, at St. Louis, when Hoekstra scored the winning goal in a 2–1 triumph.

Meanwhile, Philadelphians eagerly awaited the world premiere of the Flyers at the Spectrum. The date was October 19, 1967. The opponents were the Pittsburgh Penguins.

It was a game that almost never began because the Flyers didn't have tickets to get into the rink. An hour before game time Bill Sutherland and four of his teammates approached the players' entrance on the lower level and were abruptly stopped by a large man attired in a splendid blue uniform.

"Ticket please," the usher requested.

The players stared at one another like so many Jack Bennys awaiting the punch line. There was one, of course, but it wasn't funny. "I'm sorry," said the man, "but I can't let *anybody* in without a ticket."

Sutherland explained that he was a member of the Flyers and that the usher simply was carrying his devotion to orders a bit too far. But the large man was unmoved even after Flyers president Bill Putnam and Myrna Snider, wife of the team's principal stockholder, tried to intercede.

Acknowledging a dead end when he saw one, Sutherland finally led his mates to another corner of the Spectrum where they found an unguarded door and then, like burglars, stole through the cavernous passageways down to their new dressing room.

"That usher," said John Brogan of *The Bulletin,* "threatened Philadelphia's first major league hockey game in 37 years."

Ironically, Putnam was concerned that not enough people would pass through the Spectrum turnstiles. The rink's capacity was 14,558 seats; hopefully at least three-quarters of them would be filled at faceoff time. Putnam, himself, predicted a crowd of 12,000.

The official count was 7812 and Putnam agreed he had been misled. "They told me this was a gate town," he explained. "I don't know what happened but we sure didn't do much business at the gate tonight."

Putnam revealed that the Flyers had a 6000 advance sale for the opener, which meant they sold 1812 tickets at the box office. "I'm disappointed," said Putnam, "but not discouraged. Some of the other new teams haven't been drawing too well, but I feel we'll all eventually make it."

Another source of criticism was the price scale ($2–$5.50) which had been criticized as too high. NHL President Clarence Campbell, who attended the opening game, defended the admission structure as only he can. "We have a luxury product," he said. "To present a luxury product, we must charge luxury prices. We do not have any 60,000-seat arenas such as they do in football."

None of the 7812 cash customers seemed to mind their outlay once the puck was dropped. They immediately took to the orange-and-white jerseyed skaters and cheered them on as the game moved into the third period without a score.

While the overhead clock ticked toward the three minute mark, Rochefort unleashed a long shot at Pittsburgh's tall, thin Les Binkley. Just as Binkley blocked the drive, Sutherland cruised in front of the net and flipped the puck past the Penguins' goaltender on the rebound.

"The puck came right to me," recalls Sutherland. "Binkley was down so I just shot it over him. My linemates (Hoekstra and Rochefort) did all the work and I just tipped it in."

Given a one goal lead, the Flyers' Favell then blocked the

best shots the Penguins had to offer and won the game for Philadelphia, 1–0. Curiously, the hero was Sutherland, the man who almost didn't get past the Spectrum usher.

"I was nearly barred from my own party," Sutherland said in the jubilant Flyers' dressing room.

The victory was just the tonic needed by the Flyers. Because their next opponents were the Oakland Seals, the team that had clobbered them in the season's first game. This time the Flyers came out on top, 5–2.

But could they handle established clubs? In their first such meeting Philadelphia lost, 3–1, to the Red Wings. Still, they looked good losing and a week later jetted up to Montreal where they stunned the hockey world by handing the vaunted Canadiens a 4–1 drubbing at the Forum. Exactly a week later the Flyers invaded Boston, home of the big, bad Bruins and, thanks to Sutherland's clutch goal, defeated Bobby Orr's club, 4–2.

It was evident that Poile and Allen had built not only a respectable team but one that appeared quite capable of winning the West Division championship and the Clarence Campbell Bowl.

As the season unfolded, the Flyers worst enemy became their own home rink, the Spectrum.

12/

The Roof Falls in on a Championship Season

After a few tours of the circuit the Flyers established a reputation as a "good-field-no-hit" hockey team. Their defense was not quite airtight but it wasn't porous and the young goalkeepers were so good that established teams began making trade overtures for Parent and Favell before the 1967–68 season was half over.

That was the "good-field" aspect of the Flyers. The "no-hit" was their inability to develop the kind of scoring punch such teams as the Bruins, Canadiens, and Rangers boasted. In this regard, Philadelphia had the same problem as the other five expansion sextets.

"We don't have the big scorers to help us," said defenseman Van Impe. "We have to work for every win. When I was with Chicago last year, it was different. We had Bobby Hull and Stan Mikita to come up with the big goals and make it easier for the rest of us."

Yet with a seasoned pro like Van Impe guiding them, the

Flyers climbed to the top of the West Division and showed more spunk than some of the established clubs. Early in the season they acquired 39-year-old defenseman Larry Zeidel and he responded by playing superbly, scoring the go-ahead goal in a key 9–1 victory over Los Angeles on New Year's Eve at the Spectrum. This gave the Flyers a commendable 17–12–5 record.

What was the winning formula? Allen's coaching was crisp and insightful. He got to his men and they were willing to skate for him.

"This is a team without stars," observed Van Impe. "We're a bunch of solid, average hockey players who are willing to work hard for first place. On top of that we have two of the best goalies in the business."

Success in those early months was not without its detractors. Critics from established NHL cities mocked the expansion clubs. They talked about the dilution of the game and made it seem that the Flyers' climb to first place was less than an accomplishment. The players, naturally, bridled at such comments.

"The fact that we're an expansion team doesn't cheapen the feeling that we're on top," said Van Impe. "Expansion was a good thing for hockey. These teams are good teams. There were a lot of good hockey players around who never got a chance until this year.

"It's hard to imagine that until 1967 there were only 120 spots open for major league hockey players. Now it's 240. Expansion hasn't hurt. These guys are proving they belonged. Naturally, when I learned that Chicago had left me unprotected it was a blow to my pride. My feelings were hurt. Now I look back and I'm grateful."

Philadelphia hockey fans were equally grateful for the fine entertainment being delivered by the Flyers. The team appeared to have a lock on first place and all seemed rosy. And then the roof fell in on them. Literally.

In mid-February 1968, during a performance of the Ice Capades, high winds tore a huge hole in the top of the Spectrum at the Broad Street side of the building. The hole was estimated to be 150 feet long running north–south and 50-feet wide.

Although 11,000 spectators were in the building at the time, no serious injuries were reported and, shortly thereafter, repairs were made. But on March 1, 1968, the roof collapsed again and the building was closed indefinitely following an inspection tour by Mayor James Tate together with other city and Spectrum officials.

This presented serious problems for the Flyers who had a home game scheduled for March 3 against the Oakland Seals. The Spectrum remained shuttered and the Flyers agreed to play the "home" game that Sunday afternoon at Madison Square Garden in New York.

About 2000 fans journeyed from Philadelphia to see the matinee oddity but they were outshouted by the New Yorkers in attendance who, for inexplicable reasons, cheered loudly for the Seals. The game ended in a 1–1 tie and the Flyers yearned for the friendly confines of the Spectrum once more. Little did they know that their problems were just beginning.

Repairs on the arena roof were nowhere in sight and the problem was turning into a political football as well as a hockey headache. "We've had a battalion of inspectors storming through there ever since parts of the roof blew off," said Flyers manager Poile. "The roof has been patched but now the politicians have got into the act. They could close the place up for the balance of the season and turn us into NHL nomads."

The Flyers were bitter about the hostile treatment they had received in New York and were dubious about playing any more "home" games in foreign rinks. "We won't go back to New York," declared Poile, "unless it's for the Stanley Cup finals."

On March 7, 1968, the Flyers were scheduled to play the Bruins in Philadelphia but they still hadn't gotten the green light on the Spectrum so, this time, "home" ice was Maple Leaf Gardens in Toronto.

Poile and Allen were worried. With the Spectrum for their home games, finishing first would be a cinch. But now Los Angeles and Minnesota were closing in on them, both being only two points behind.

By now the Flyers were in trouble. Big trouble. The Bruins not only beat them, 2–1, in Toronto but their veteran defenseman Larry Zeidel engaged Eddie Shack of Boston in a wild and bloody stick-swinging match. Referee Bruce Hood gave each player a match misconduct penalty which carried an automatic $100 fine.

"It was one of the worst stick fights I ever saw," remembers Frank Udvari, eastern supervisor of officials for the NHL.

This was just the beginning of an angry exchange of charges made by Zeidel and other Flyer officials against the Bruins. "I don't know why," said Poile, "but the whole Boston club is after Larry. They told him they were going to get him earlier in the season. I reported it to the league but they did nothing about it. This was the result."

In time Zeidel and Shack were suspended by NHL President Campbell for four and three games, respectively. The Flyers were fading fast. And Ed Van Impe realized that the tailspin had to be corrected before the team not only blew first place but also a playoff berth. "If we get our spirit back," Van Impe commented, "we'll bust out of this thing."

If Philadelphia was going to turn the tide it would have to happen against the pursuing North Stars on March 10, 1968, at the Metropolitan Sports Center in Bloomington, Minnesota. Before the game Van Impe delivered a pep talk to his men.

"We lost to the Bruins the other night," he said, "but I know we're starting to come; we're getting our spirit back. All we have to do now is get a few goals and we'll be off and running. We're getting the shots but they're not going in. Once they start, watch out!"

That night the Flyers put two goals into the North Stars net and kept Minnesota from scoring any themselves. The tide had turned.

"They may have put us out of the Spectrum," Van Impe noted, "but we're not going to let that bother us. We're still going to win this thing for the fans of Philadelphia."

Meanwhile, the Spectrum roof situation had gone from ridiculous to downright absurd. There was no sign of the job being completed by mid-March and the bedouin Flyers remained on the road. WHERE, OH WHERE ARE OUR WANDERING BOYS TONIGHT? asked a headline in *The Bulletin*.

"Our situation is embarrassing to the league," said Flyers president Bill Putnam. "Everybody is hurt by it, including the players."

And the fans.

If there was any doubt that the Flyers, in their few months of existence, had developed a loyal following these doubts were now put to rest. On March 16, 1968, more than 300 Flyer rooters stormed Philadelphia's City Hall demanding that the Spectrum roof be repaired promptly so their team could return.

Reporter William Storm of *The Bulletin* described them as "well-dressed, orderly and jolly. Many were accompanied by children, some in baby carriages."

The picketing, which began at 1 P.M., was led by telephone repairman John Wagner, president of the Flyers' Fan Club, and his wife Cheryl. Signs carried messages proclaiming: PLEASE BRING OUR FLYERS HOME. PASS THE PUCK, NOT THE BUCK. And BIG WINDS BLEW THE ROOF OFF THE SPECTRUM. NOW THE BIG WINDS WON'T FIX IT.

By now the Spectrum roof was a *cause célèbre* from Broad Street to Brickerville. Columnist Sandy Grady visited the arena and filed this report: "A cold wind blew across the empty parking lot. The Spectrum was dark and deserted. It looked like a children's plaything, broken and forgotten now that Christmas was over with nobody interested in putting the pieces together."

All the pressure finally began to produce results and a faint hope arose that the building might be reopened in time for the Stanley Cup playoffs. Meantime the Flyers, inspired by Van Impe, reeled off four wins and a tie in five games to rejuvenate their drive for first place.

Playing out of a suitcase had become a ritual and they regarded the Spectrum as a distant, though beloved, relative. Whenever a club official or newsman rejoined the team on the road, one of the Flyers would surely ask: "What's new with the arena?" Or, "Do you think we'll be able to have the playoffs at home?"

Bill Putnam was under fire from the NHL office which demanded to know by March 25, 1968, whether or not the playoffs could be held in Philadelphia. But when the day passed with still no answer, Putnam won an extension.

"At this point," Putnam admitted, "I don't know whether I'm optimistic or pessimistic. Our playoff tickets are printed and will go on sale immediately if we get an okay from the Spectrum and the scientists who are supposed to test the roof."

With four games remaining on their schedule, the Flyers still were being closely pursued by the Los Angeles Kings. "I'm still confident we'll finish first," said manager Poile, "although the travel has really hurt our players. If Los Angeles wins all three of its games, we'll win all four of ours."

On March 27, the Flyers skated against the Blues at St. Louis and lost, 3–0. Their next game was a "home" affair to be played the following night at *Le Colisée* in Quebec City. This was the most important match of the season for Philadelphia. A victory would assure them of no worse than a first-place tie with Los Angeles no matter how many games the Kings won; it would also mean that each member of the Flyers could obtain $2250 as his share of the first-place loot offered by the league.

Defeating the Blues would be a difficult chore. St. Louis started ace goaltender Glenn Hall who was enjoying an excellent season with his new team. The Flyers went with Doug Favell, whom they had selected over Hall in the 1967 expansion draft. "This team has a lot of heart," assured a proud Van Impe. "We're going to play as hard as we can to wrap this thing up once and for all."

The 5382 spectators at *Le Colisée* were treated to an outstanding exhibition of goaltending by Hall in the first period. Time and again he blunted the Flyers' most dangerous shots and the teams left the ice after 20 minutes of play, tied 0–0.

Once the second period began, the Flyers sent wave after wave over the St. Louis blue line shooting for the lead. Finally, the line of Forbes Kennedy, Claude Laforge, and Gary Dornhoefer barged into the Blues' territory. Kennedy controlled the puck behind the net, looking for an unguarded teammate.

"All I could see," Kennedy later explained, "was a pair of orange socks in front of Hall. I didn't know who they belonged to, but I figured the guy must be on our side, so I passed to him."

The socks belonged to Dornhoefer who had riveted himself to a spot directly in front of the St. Louis net. He watched the puck skitter out to him across the goal mouth and slammed the rubber past Hall at 4:21 of the period. "Forbes and Claude did all the work on that one," said Dornhoefer. "They set me up perfectly. All I had to do was put it in."

Now it was up to Favell to keep them out and that he did throughout the second period and well into the third. But with six minutes remaining the Blues found a chink in the Flyers' defensive armor. Larry Keenan, a dangerous scorer, fought his way past the Philadelphia defenders and confronted Favell one-on-one.

Keenan had freed himself enough from his pursuers to

have an option to either try a *deke* (an elaborate, close-in faking maneuver) on Favell or simply release a hard shot to either corner.

Keenan shot and Favell kept his eyes trained on the puck throughout its short and speedy flight toward the corner of the net. At the last split-second, the goalie's arm flailed out and the puck bounced harmlessly to the side. "I got it with my stick," Favell later explained. "No, I wasn't worried."

The big save did the trick. Philadelphia scored one more goal to win the game, 2–0, and began icing the champagne for what they hoped would be a victory celebration after their next match, against the Pittsburgh Penguins.

"Now," manager Poile noted, "I like the odds."

A happy Van Impe laughed. "Things might have looked a little bleak this morning but they're sure a lot brighter now."

The Flyers *had* won the big one while the Kings salvaged only one tie in their final three games. When Los Angeles tied Oakland 2–2 in the Kings' final game of the season, Philadelphia became the first champions of the West Division.

Although deprived of winning the Clarence Campbell Bowl on their home ice, the Flyers did have the satisfaction of being in Pennsylvania when the news flashed that they were the West Division winners.

At 1:30 A.M. on March 31, 1968, most of the Philadelphia players were in their hotel rooms when the report arrived that Oakland had tied Los Angeles, 2–2, with 15 minutes to play. The Flyers' brass adjourned to owner Ed Snider's hotel suite where a long-distance call was placed to Oakland. The telephone operator then provided Flyers' officials and Philadelphia newsmen with a play-by-play of the final 40 seconds.

"It's all over," shouted a newsman, "you're the champs."

Snider refused to believe it. A call was made to United Press International for verification. A UPI night man checked the sports wire and noticed that a bulletin from Oakland was clicking off the teletype machine. He took one look at it and picked up the phone again.

"You can start celebrating right now!"

Not everybody was prepared to celebrate. At his moment of triumph Poile was horizontal, trying to stop a bloody nose. But other members of the hierarchy roared their approval. Snider and Putnam embraced and, one by one, the players began demonstrating their jubilation.

"I know there are going to be ups and downs for as long as we're playing hockey," said center Lou Angotti. "But when you take everything into consideration, whatever happens after this will have to rank second to what's happened this season.

"It wasn't just worrying about first place, but also wondering where our next game would be played. Why, we'd get up some mornings feeling seedy and not know what the heck was going on because we were on the move all the time. We'll certainly be glad to get home for the playoffs."

Almost simultaneously came the news that the Spectrum was ready and waiting.

The first-place celebrations took on many forms. Ed Snider opened a bottle of champagne and offered a toast: "Here's to the greatest team in the world. The Stanley Cup is next!"

Defenseman John Miszuk opened a bottle of wine for his teammates in front of the hotel while they awaited taxicabs to take them to the Artists & Photographers Club for a private party.

"Did we have to win it right now?" asked goalie Favell.

"I just took three sleeping pills and 'The Slime People' is the late movie."

So the party that not even the Spectrum roof could ruin roared on through the night. The team that had to play 14 out of its last 14 games on the road during a homestretch run for the championship laughed and cried and shouted and laughed some more as only a gutsy club deserved to after so rare an ordeal.

"I said a few weeks ago," Van Impe remarked, "that we wanted to win this championship for the fans who have stood behind us in Philadelphia. Now we want nothing more than to win a couple of playoff series, maybe even the Stanley Cup, for them."

It was a noble thought and the first challenge would come in Round One from the St. Louis Blues, a team that had been coming on strong during the last half of the schedule. An easy enough challenge to Flyers' fans who welcomed their heroes home, but the Philadelphia players sensed an extremely difficult battle ahead.

"We'll play as hard as we can," Van Impe concluded, "for as long as we can."

13/

Build-up to a Letdown

The Clarence Campbell Bowl was not exactly a bowl of cherries for the Flyers. They finished the season losing 5–1 to the Pittsburgh Penguins and, in so doing, fell below the .500 mark with a season total of 31 victories, 32 defeats, and 11 ties. The loss to Pittsburgh left a bad taste in the typewriters of critics such as John Brogan of *The Bulletin.*

"The Flyers," wrote Brogan, "finished their season in a most unglorious manner. They stunk out the Pittsburgh Civic Arena."

Ed Conrad, writing in *The Philadelphia Daily News,* was more sympathetic. "The Flyers," said Conrad, "could not get up for the game simply because, win or lose, they had clinched the West Division title."

Several valid arguments were made for the Flyers' flat finish. They had been on the road for almost the entire month of March. They were tired and they were saving themselves for the playoffs.

"We have nothing to be ashamed of," defended manager Poile. "Not one thing. Sure we would have liked to finish off better than we did, but we're still the champs, aren't we? We have 73 points and that's more than anyone else in the division. That must mean we're the best team."

Then, Poile got to the matter which would prove to be of utmost importance in the weeks to come. "Right now," he went on, "this team has had it. It's beat. All this travel has everyone worn out. You can't play 21 of your last 24 games on the road and not feel it. But this team did it and won a championship as well. No one else in any sport has ever done that. The players deserve a lot of credit."

What remained to be seen was whether the Flyers could rev themselves up again after the final game letdown. But when they returned to the Spectrum to prepare for their opening round series still another black cloud roiled into view bringing trouble.

The latest calamity was revealed at the Flyers' pre-play-offs workout when a grey-haired goalie with a middle-aged pot belly took his place in front of the net normally guarded by the agile Doug Favell. It was Stu Nahan, Philadelphia's play-by-play announcer, who raised the question: what happened to Favell?

"We sent him to the hospital," replied coach Allen. "He wasn't feeling well when he reported this morning, so we sent him for an examination."

Philadelphia was favored over St. Louis in the best-of-seven series which opened at the Spectrum on April 4, 1968. But every one of the Flyers realized that St. Louis was not a team to be taken lightly. The Blues had Glenn Hall, a veteran of many Stanley Cup playoffs, in goal and such Cup-hardened veterans as Dickie Moore and Doug Harvey, who had played on several Montreal championship teams.

Besides, the Blues were a genuinely tough hockey club and a bigger team than the Flyers. With such robust defensemen as Bob and Barclay Plager and Noel Picard, the Blues could be expected to try intimidation on the Philadelphians to soften up such smaller Flyers as Andre Lacroix and Lou Angotti.

The Flyers were greeted with a tumultuous ovation when they stepped on Spectrum ice for the first time since February 29 when they played Los Angeles. But once the opening playoff game began the fans had little to cheer about. Jim Roberts scored for St. Louis and nobody scored for the Flyers. The final score was 1–0 and those fears of the end-of-season letdown were confirmed. Philadelphia needed a win badly in Game Two at the Spectrum if they expected to stay alive in the series.

The Flyers stayed alive, but just barely. A goal by Leon Rochefort enabled them to narrowly eke out a 4–3 triumph and tie the series at one apiece. "The difference between the first game and the second game," said Pat Hannigan, "was only a step or a half-step. This time we got to the puck first. That's all there was to it."

Still, it was not an encouraging win and the Flyers embarked for St. Louis more demoralized than hopeful about the next two games at the Blues' Arena. On April 10, St. Louis confirmed these suspicions by defeating the Flyers 3–2 on Larry Keenan's overtime goal and then winning the fourth game 5–2 for a three games to one advantage.

All of a sudden, the once-favored Flyers were on the ropes and staggered home to Philadelphia for what loomed as the coup de grace on April 13. As feared, the bigger Blues were flexing their muscle.

"We have to stand up to them," warned defenseman Larry Zeidel. "They outfought us in St. Louis. They think that with a stick in their hands they're ten feet tall. We have to cut them down to size. We must go after them."

The Flyers took Zeidel's advice and went after the Blues with a vengeance. They mounted a 3–0 lead in the first period, scored once in the second period and twice in the third. Final score: Philadelphia 6, St. Louis 1. But the score was almost secondary to a prolonged bout of bloodletting that took place midway in the third period.

According to most observers the war began when Noel Picard, a huge former tavern-bouncer, took on the smaller Claude Laforge of the Flyers. Picard flattened Laforge who left the ice for 14 stitches in the mouth.

"Picard hit Laforge from behind," manager Poile insisted. "That doesn't take much guts. That punch may just have won the series for us."

Whatever else it did, the punch inspired players from both benches to pour over the boards like infantrymen rushing from their trenches. And what followed for the next 20 minutes was sheer mayhem, as battles erupted all over the ice.

"Some claimed it was the greatest fight in hockey history," observed Hugh Brown of *The Bulletin*. "Older hands who had read Herbert Asbury's book *The Gangs of New York* claimed that except for the absence of blackjacks and knuckledusters it had to be something like the historical battle of the Erie Basin Hellcats and the Hudson Dusters."

Typical was the reaction of Flyers' goalie Doug Favell who wasn't even in the game. Watching the action from the bench, Favell leaped over the boards when he saw Picard put the slug on Laforge.

"I was going after Picard," said Favell, "but on the way Dickie Moore challenged me. I said I didn't want to have anything to do with him, but Moore came at me and we had it out."

As far as could be determined only one person in the audience of 10,587 took a dim view of the proceedings. That was NHL President Clarence Campbell who was in the press box assiduously taking notes on the disorder.

Campbell had been viewing the lack of decorum between the Blues and Flyers with growing concern, particularly after Gary Dornhoefer suffered a compound fracture of the right leg during a fight with Barclay Plager in an earlier game. The charges and countercharges flowing from one front office to the other were becoming increasingly bitter. Blues' coach Scotty Bowman was trading twits with Poile while Bill Putnam and St. Louis owner Sid Salomon, Jr., were not exactly friends.

However, Campbell was more concerned with the riot-a-game pattern that had been developing. "In the first game of the series in which the players of both teams came off the benches it was a St. Louis player who came off the bench first," said Campbell. "On the second and third occasions there is no doubt that the Flyers left first."

Based on this reasoning, Campbell fined Flyers' coach Keith Allen $500 and Blues' coach Scotty Bowman $400. "Any further default on their part for the remainder of the playoffs will produce more severe disciplinary action," warned Campbell.

The player rioting, which proved to be the first shots in what has developed into a bitter inter-city rivalry, brought on considerable penalties. Campbell levied $100 fines against eleven St. Louis players. And similar fines were given to the Flyers' Joe Watson, Jean Gauthier, Lou Angotti, Leon Rochefort, Brit Selby, Bill Sutherland, Andre Lacroix, Ed Hoekstra, and Larry Zeidel. In addition, goalie Favell received a $150 fine for persisting in several fights after they had been broken up.

Manager Poile was furious. "He (Campbell) made a mistake—his second one this year," snapped Poile. "His first mistake was Zeidel."

Coach Allen was more discreet, despite his $500 fine. "I don't want to say anything until I talk to Campbell," said Allen.

As a precautionary move, the Flyers hired two off-duty Philadelphia policemen and flew them to St. Louis to guard their dressing room. Poile insisted that they would be unarmed during the sixth game on April 16, 1968, which, of course, could be the Flyers' last meet of the season.

"There's no tomorrow if we lose," said Bernie Parent who got the goaltending assignment. "But if we win we'll beat them in the seventh game in Philadelphia."

Parent was carrying a hot hand for the Flyers. He had played superbly during the 6–1 triumph and had reduced his goals-against average to 1.47, best of any goalie in the series.

"This will be a pressure game," Parent added, "and I know I'll be nervous before it begins. However, it'll only be from the time we go on the ice for the pre-game warmup until St. Louis takes its first shot of the game. After that, it won't bother me a bit."

The Blues shot hard and often in the first period before a win-thirsty crowd of 13,738 at St. Louis Arena. As promised, Parent appeared jittery until the opening shot delivered by the Blues. Then he settled into a near-flawless pattern of splits, lunges, and diving saves that stopped all but one St. Louis drive. At 18:06 of the first period, with the Flyers' Forbes Kennedy in the penalty box, Gerry Melnyk deflected Barclay Plager's long shot past Parent.

Melnyk's score grew larger and larger as the second period progressed and Blues' goalie Glenn Hall exchanged spectacular saves with Parent. The Flyers could not foil the old master and left the ice down 1–0 after two periods. In a sense the Flyers were lucky to be behind by only one goal. St. Louis had outshot Philadelphia 16–3 in the middle period not to mention a lengthy two-man advantage which was alternately thwarted by the sterling penalty-killing of Ed Van Impe, Jimmy Johnson, Bill Sutherland, and Ed Hoekstra.

But as the third period unfolded the Flyers' defensive assets were becoming more and more insignificant since they were unable to score a goal. St. Louis rooters sensed the killing and as the final minute of the third period ticked away they delivered a standing ovation to the nearly victorious Blues. However, they had not bargained for the Flyers' heart.

Although the Philadelphia sextet had been unable to gain a faceoff in deep St. Louis territory, they persisted in their attempts to get a shot at Hall. Parent had been removed from the Flyers' net for a sixth attacker and the last, desperate assaults were mounted.

Dickie Moore of the Blues thwarted the first one at center ice. He snared the puck and the onetime NHL leading scorer flung the rubber at the gaping net. It slid to the right of the goalpost, missing by a matter of inches, and the Flyers were still alive with precious few seconds remaining.

Hoekstra went back for the puck and started what would have to be the team's last offensive of the third period, if not the campaign. He danced around two St. Louis defenders who vainly tried to spear the puck off his stick and suddenly found some skating room as he approached the red line.

It was then that he spotted Rochefort free near center ice and skimmed a pass to his linemate who sped over the St. Louis blue line. Rochefort's shot was easily handled by Hall but the goalkeeper could not muzzle the rebound which was grabbed by Sutherland.

By now the Flyers had positioned themselves entirely inside the Blues' zone as if in power play formation. Sutherland looked up and noticed Van Impe standing alone at the right point, 50 feet away. The pass was true and the slick-haired defenseman powered a long shot at Hall as the clock recorded the last 20 seconds of the period.

Hall followed the trajectory of the drive, hoping that it wouldn't carom off a body and suddenly change course before he could reach it. As the shot arrived, Hall carefully fell in front of it and prevented the puck from going past him but, once again, he was unable to smother it.

Tiny Andre Lacroix had positioned himself near the left corner of the net. The puck bounced directly to his stick and with 15 seconds remaining Philadelphia had tied the score.

"It's obvious," wrote Jack Chevalier of *The Inquirer*, "somebody up there is madly in love with the Flyers, a hockey team kissed by destiny itself."

But destiny's rewards were yet to come. The sixth game

had now gone into sudden-death overtime, the first score being the winner. Philadelphia had the emotional momentum but the Flyers would have to quickly capitalize on it in the first overtime period. They tried, hurling 14 shots at Hall, but they failed and the teams remained tied, 1–1, as the second overtime began.

"The Flyers," Chevalier observed, "had lost their momentum."

They also seemed about to lose the game as the Blues sent volley after volley at the frequently abandoned Parent. Just past the ten minute mark St. Louis center Red Berenson assaulted the Flyers' net on a dangerous two-on-one break. His shot was hard and true but Parent, equal to the occasion, batted it aside.

Now it was Philadelphia's turn. The Flyers tried to penetrate the enemy defense but were met by a wall of blue-shirted skaters just inside the St. Louis zone. Don Blackburn of the Flyers had the puck and, unable to find a free teammate, decided to take a long, seemingly hopeless, shot.

"Everybody was around the blue line," Blackburn recalled, "and I didn't have a play. So I just slipped a shot at Hall."

It was a backhander without much pizazz; but it was on target and it did have an ominous enough quality about it to still the entire Arena while flying goalward. "Nobody even moved," said Blackburn, "until the red light went on."

Hall was beaten when the fluke shot bounced on its side and took a bizarre swerve past the St. Louis goalie just as he prepared to smother it with his mitt.

Bedlam engulfed the Philadelphia bench and the Flyer

players on the ice. "Lacroix and Blackburn were nearly pummelled to death," wrote Chevalier, "by their joyous teammates."

The series was tied at three apiece. The Flyers were on the verge of setting a league record; no team ever had come from behind a 1–3 deficit in Stanley Cup play to win the series. Everything would be decided on April 18, 1968, at the Spectrum.

Although only sensed at the time, the Flyers' fate was already sealed a few nights earlier when the Blues' Kansas City farm team had been eliminated from the Central League playoffs. This meant that St. Louis could promote skaters from their farm team for the final game and one of them was Kansas City player–coach Doug Harvey. "Harvey," said Blues' coach Scotty Bowman, "is probably the greatest defenseman of all time."

Flyers' coach Allen was inclined to agree with Bowman and went about the business of preparing his men for the Harvey challenge. "He's 43 years old," said Allen at the pregame meeting. "He's good but he's no kid anymore either. We have to make him skate, to tire his old legs."

As in the sixth game St. Louis scored first in the opening period. Frank St. Marseille beat Parent with a 25-foot shot and the Spectrum crowd of 14,646 fell silent as their heroes once again found it difficult to respond against Glenn Hall.

Meanwhile, the Flyers did their best to harass the supercool Harvey and at 17:01 he was whistled off the ice for hooking. The Spectrum immediately came alive and so did the Flyers. Andre Lacroix, hero of the sixth game, fired the puck at Hall who was partially blocked by Bill Sutherland standing with his back to Lacroix.

The puck threaded its way through Sutherland's legs, hit his stick, and curved past Hall. It now was up to the Flyers to capitalize on their momentum and the encouragement of the home fans. Time and again the Philadelphians threatened to light the red bulb behind Hall but, just as often, they were thwarted either by the goalie or the seasoned St. Louis defense, led by Harvey, a seven-time winner of the Norris Trophy as the NHL's best defenseman.

Ironically, on the day of the game Harvey had been needled by his 18-year-old son who had phoned him from Montreal. "He told me to take a seat on the end of the bench," said Harvey, "so he could see me on TV. Once I heard that I knew I *had* to play a good game."

With each passing minute of the second period the Flyers were becoming less and less able to contain Harvey and at 10:45 he managed to get the puck to Larry Keenan who was camped ten feet in front of Parent. Keenan's shot beat Parent, skittered through his legs but, miraculously, hit the goalpost.

Both the goalie and defenseman Zeidel wildly hurled themselves at the loose puck which bounced off Zeidel's skate and then off Parent's stick into the Philadelphia net. The time was 10:45 of the second period and the Flyers were in trouble because Hall and Harvey were providing St. Louis with an impregnable defense.

"Doug," said Keith Allen, "was giving them a steadying influence. And he blocked a lot of shots. He always seemed to get a piece of the puck."

Harvey, in turn, began skating like a man possessed, as if determined to win the game single-handedly for his club. "This game meant a lot to me," he admitted later. "I wanted to prove that I could still play in the NHL."

117

There was no doubt in the Flyers' minds that Harvey belonged. "He played like a football safety man," wrote Jack Chevalier, "hanging back on defense to make sure the Flyers didn't get clear shots at Hall."

The Spectrum rooters pinned their faint hopes on a repeat of the sixth game miracle: a last-minute goal after Parent was called to the bench for a sixth skater. The decisive face-off was held with 54 seconds remaining on the clock at a point outside the St. Louis blue line, 110 feet from the Philadelphia goal crease.

Lou Angotti took the faceoff for the Flyers and Red Berenson for the Blues. Using his elongated stick—the longest in the NHL—Berenson easily won the draw and, in the same motion, lifted the puck toward the Flyers' cage.

"I was trying to get it down to their end," said Berenson. "With the goalie out I knew I had a chance to score."

Berenson's shot drifted lazily toward the empty net as the Flyers, all out of position to get back in time, grimly watched it bulge the twine at 19:10 of the period. "I probably couldn't make that shot again in ten tries," Berenson admitted.

This once was enough to burst the Flyers' bubble and 50 seconds later the Philadelphians were lined up at center ice pumping the hands of the victorious Blues. The build-up to a letdown was complete. Winners of the Clarence Campbell Bowl, the first-place Flyers were drained of energy by their tedious month on the road. Yet they had still managed to take the fresher, more experienced Blues as far as was humanly possible.

"It was a trying year," said president Putnam. "But all things considered, it was a good one."

14/

Heartbreak

A favorite summer pastime for Philadelphia sports fans in 1968 was arguing about the success—or failure—of the Flyers, both artistically and financially.

The seven-game loss to St. Louis was "a downer," as they say on Broad Street, that clouded the Flyers' future on the Clarence Campbell Bowl. At the time, the Stanley Cup was out of the question.

Then there was the vital matter of attendance. It wasn't very good but, then again, it wasn't very bad. In 30 home dates before the roof blew off the Spectrum the Flyers attracted 298,757 paying customers. During the playoffs they drew 46,933 for the four home games. Putnam was at once happy and disconsolate about developments.

"At the beginning of the year," the Flyers' president allowed, "I projected the season on a break-even basis. About December 1st that all changed. Our attendance wasn't as good as I figured it would be early in the season. But after December things began to look really bright. Then, the roof fell in."

The Flyers lost approximately $300,000 their first season.

On paper it looked bad, but on the street Philadelphians were talking hockey and clearly had adopted the once-bedouin Flyers as the new sports darlings of the town. "In time," Putnam accurately predicted, "the Philadelphia franchise will be one of the best in hockey."

Manager Poile was aware that his team needed more scoring punch and at least one more big hitter. During the off-season he announced that he was promoting an All-French line from the Flyers' Quebec Aces farm team in the American League. The three players were Jean-Guy Gendron, who had previous NHL experience with the New York Rangers, Simon Nolet, and Andre Lacroix, who had been promoted during the previous season.

For beef, there was Ralph MacSweyn, a bulky defenseman who liked to hit people. "MacSweyn," said Poile, "is the most improved hockey player in the organization. He's a throwback to the old days. He hits you at center ice."

The Flyers opened the 1968–69 season, losing 3–2 to Boston and proceeded downhill from there. They lost three out of their first four games and, as frequently happens with professional teams, the losses bred dissension.

Larry Zeidel, who had played such a vital part in the Flyers' rookie year, was inexplicably benched and eventually demoted to Quebec. When he refused to report to the American League club Poile suspended him.

"He (Zeidel) hasn't been playing much," said Poile, "so I asked him to go down to Quebec for two weeks to get in shape. I didn't ask him to take a cut in salary or anything like that. I just asked him to go down for two weeks."

But Zeidel, a physical culture buff, was in shape and his teammates all knew that he had one of the best defensive records on the team when he played regularly. Zeidel's refusal to go down to the minors was quietly endorsed by his sympathetic teammates and the seeds of the anti-Poile movement had been planted.

By early December critics realized that there was no way the Flyers would repeat their first-place finish of the previous year. On December 4, 1968, they were defeated, 3–1, in Los Angeles and on December 6 they were humiliated, 4–0, by Oakland. All eyes were on Poile who was being asked to solve the Philadelphia problem.

"I know what's wrong with this team," he commented. "It doesn't have the zip it had last year. It doesn't have the spark. We need that one big gun. One player could ignite this whole team. That's all we need—one big gun. But how do you get him? If I could come up with that answer it would solve a lot of problems."

Flyer fans urged Poile to make a trade. The Maple Leafs suggested a deal which would send Brit Selby to Toronto for Bill Sutherland who had played for the Flyers in 1967–68 but had been claimed by the Leafs in the 1968 draft. Poile was not amused by the offer.

"That's about the 88th time I've been insulted in the past few weeks," he snorted. "They offer their sixth defenseman for our first, or their 12th forward for our best. What can be gained by making a trade like that?"

The way Poile explained it, the problem was not in the front office but rather in the Flyers' dressing room. That intangible element was gone. "What puzzles me," added the manager, "is why some of these players who were here last year don't seem to have the same enthusiasm. We gave them all good raises and I think we've treated them well."

On the other hand, the Flyers treated their customers well and not so well by turns. One night they were beaten, 8–0, by St. Louis before an insulted Spectrum crowd which saw Red Berenson of the Blues pump six goals past goalie Doug Favell.

"The most amazing thing about Red's performance," said St. Louis goalie Jacques Plante, "was that he didn't get one cheap goal. Every one was a good, clean shot." Berenson's sixth score tied a modern record which had been set by Syd Howe of Detroit. The only solace for Spectrum fans was that the Flyers prevented Red from scoring a seventh and record-breaking goal.

"They weren't about to let me set a record," said Berenson. "They were all over me after the sixth goal. The last time I went down the ice Van Impe nearly chopped my leg off."

The game only cost the Flyers two points, but psychologically it upset the team as a whole and goalie Favell in particular. "Just say he was great and I was lousy," offered Favell after the disaster. "I don't want to say another word."

Significantly, Favell's goals-against average soared from a commendable 2.27 in his rookie season to 3.56 in the 1968–69 campaign, the year of the Berenson barrage.

Suspending Zeidel obviously wasn't the answer to the Flyers' problems any more than the elevation of the All-French line. The 8–0 St. Louis debacle was repeated later in the campaign when Detroit bombed the Flyers 9–1 on February 23, 1969. President Putnam was losing patience with his front office and Poile knew it. After the Detroit debacle, Poile bade farewell to a Philadelphia newsman, sounding as if it was his last hurrah.

"I'm going on a trip," said Poile, "and I may not be back. I've enjoyed my years in Philadelphia, though."

"The boss," added Poile, "has ordered me to do something. He says if I don't, he will."

One of Poile's dilemmas was that Putnam had learned about hockey very quickly. When Putnam had organized the Flyers he knew a lot about organization but only a little about hockey. By 1969, however, he knew a great deal about both and he particularly knew a bad game when he saw one.

"The game against Detroit," said Putnam, "was the worst hockey game I've ever seen the Flyers play. Bud and Keith had better do something. I don't know what, but so far we haven't done anything."

Poile and Allen did several things which included the preservation of their jobs. They managed to push, pull, wheedle, and cajole the Flyers into third place with a record of 20 wins, 35 losses, and 21 ties for 61 points, a far cry from their handsome first-year mark of 31–32–11–73. Only one thing about them was the same: Philadelphia's first-round opponents were the St. Louis Blues who now boasted the West Division's first superstar, Red Berenson, and a rejuvenated goalie in Jacques Plante who was playing as well as he did during his halcyon days with the Montreal Canadiens. All of which added up to disaster for the Flyers.

This time the series opened in St. Louis and the Blues just about ran the Flyers out of the rink with a 5–1 triumph. Plante took over from Glenn Hall in the second match and stopped the Flyers cold while his shooters scored five times.

The series now moved to Philadelphia where the home team tried to devise some way of stopping the elusive Red Berenson while neutralizing the intimidating Plager Brothers and Noel Picard. There appeared to be no answers and the frustration of Flyer fans was obvious when the teams took the ice for Game Three.

Banners adorned the rink and suggested the contempt Philadelphians held for Scotty Bowman and his enforcers. BUCKETMOUTH BOWMAN AND HIS THREE STOOGES was one. THE BLUES ARE BUSH was another.

As the visiting coach approached his bench, an intemperate fan leaned over and shouted, "Hey magnet head why don't you take your gorilla (Picard) and go back to the zoo."

"It's just that St. Louis is our blood rival," explained Ed Snider, the Flyers' board chairman. "The game is just so emotional it brings on these things."

One of the few to find some levity in the proceeding was St. Louis defenseman Bob Plager who suggested that Spectrum fans were chintzier than the St. Louis spectators. "At home," said Plager, "the fans have class. They throw nickels on the ice. Here it's only pennies!"

The Flyers threw very little at the St. Louis net in the two games at the Spectrum and were easily dispatched by scores of 3–0 and 4–1. So one-sided was the four-game sweep that coach Bowman was almost apologetic. "Philadelphia has a lot better team than they showed in this series," he said. "When a team loses the first two games of a seven-game series, they get down. And it's awfully difficult to get them back up again."

Philadelphia coach Allen was less compassionate. He lamented what a terribly disappointing season for himself and the team. "The playoff series," he said, "was a disaster. We didn't put anything together in the fourth game just as we didn't put anything together in the other games."

It was inevitable that heads would roll at and that new faces would be introduced to, hopefully, produce a winner. On May 19, 1969, the axe fell, but when the dust cleared nobody could find any victims. Keith Allen was promoted from coach to vice president and assistant general manager and Vic Stasiuk, coach of the Flyers' Quebec farm team, was brought in to replace Allen.

"We're not pointing fingers," said president Bill Putnam. "If we had gone to the finals, I'd venture to say we'd have made the same move."

Snider added, "There was no dissatisfaction. We were just looking in the mirror to see what we could do to improve our situation. The St. Louis Blues were first and we were third. We want to catch and surpass them and eventually build the best organization in hockey."

This was, of course, a laudible goal but the results were still some distance away. In 1969–70 the Flyers got worse. They finished fifth, out of the playoffs for the first time in the club's brief history. By December of that third year, nerves in the front office had become frazzled and friction developed, especially between club owner Snider and manager Poile. Snider fired the burly, garrulous Poile for doing a "sporadic job." His successor was his assistant, Allen.

A sphinx-like character who was generally liked around the NHL, Allen thought he had a playoff contender; but the Flyers' situation remained in doubt until the final weekend of the season and a game at the Spectrum on April 4, 1970, against the Minnesota North Stars.

Philadelphia and Minnesota were engaged in a three-way fight with Oakland for the final two playoff spots in the West Division. A loss would eliminate the Flyers or North

Stars, while a tie would leave the situation still in doubt.

Both clubs played a close-checking game, willing to settle for a tie if necessary. For two periods and seven-and-a-half minutes of the third period neither team scored. Then there was a faceoff in the Flyers zone and the puck slid along the boards to Minnesota defenseman Barry Gibbs. Almost carelessly, Gibbs moved to center ice and lofted a high, soft shot at goalie Bernie Parent.

"The shot," said writer Ray Didinger, "might have been the easiest shot Parent had seen all season—if he had seen it."

The 14,606 witnesses who saw it could not believe their eyes. Neither could Gibbs. "Parent never moved a muscle," said the North Star defenseman, "and then I saw it go in. I think when I shot, the puck must have come off (Larry) Hillman's black pants. I mean, Parent just never moved an inch."

Parent's error cost the Flyers the game, 1–0, and a playoff berth. In the dressing room the 25-year-old French-Canadian goaltender sounded like Brooklyn Dodgers' Pitcher Billy Loes after he once lost a World Series grounder in the sun.

"I never saw the puck," said Parent. "That's all. I lost it. It happens sometimes. You just lose it. It was the worst goal scored on me all year. I remember Montreal losing the Stanley Cup on a goal like that about 15 years ago, but you think it can never happen to you."

Even the usually unflappable Allen flapped a bit this time. "It's unbelievable," the manager stated. "The whole season ruined on a shot like that."

Some critics didn't feel the Flyers really deserved a playoff berth. After all, they had lost their last six consecutive games and were completely shut out for the final 144 minutes and 17 seconds of the season.

"But think of it," said Snider in the post-mortem room, holding a drink in one hand and a cigarette in the other. "Last Saturday we played a game for second place." Then a pause. "Second place. No, it's not the money. It's what you work for; what we thought we had."

Allen didn't remain despondent for long. The elimination was painful to be sure, but he genuinely liked the club he was now managing.

"We're a young club," Allen said with optimism, "and the defense is solid. I think the future is bright.

"I really think this was our best team in three years," Allen insisted. "I had a lot of confidence in it. We had more muscle and more scoring potential than last year or the year before."

No doubt he was referring to a young man who had finished fourth on the Flyers' list of scorers—Bobby Clarke—who had 15 goals and 31 assists for 46 points.

Meanwhile, front office-watchers kept an argus eye on the Spectrum awaiting further developments in what *Philadelphia Magazine* described as the Flyers' "office coup." It finally happened in June 1970 when Putnam sold his 25 percent interest and left the team. He was replaced on the NHL Board of Governors by Snider and, at long last, things seemed to be stabilized.

Which was important because with each season the Spectrum crowd was becoming more sophisticated and more demanding. "The hockey fans in Philadelphia have grown up with the team over the past four years," said Maury Levy, associate editor of *Philadelphia Magazine*. "At first, all that most of them knew was that it was good when the guys in orange put the little piece of rubber in the goal at the other end of the ice."

"Knowledge has come with time. Hockey here used to be a game of pure emotion. Now it's finesse. Now that the guys in orange have learned how to pass and shoot a lot better, the fans have become more involved in the intricacies."

The 1970–71 club was, once again, a playoff team; though a third-place outfit that had the misfortune of meeting the Chicago Black Hawks in the opening Cup round. This developed because the NHL had, with added expansion, rearranged the two divisions, placing Chicago in the West along with the Flyers.

Powered by superstars such as Bobby Hull and Stan Mikita, the Hawks had little trouble dumping the Flyers right out of the playdowns in four consecutive games: 5–2, 6–2, 3–2, 6–2.

It was disappointing to Snider and Company but not a complete tragedy—there was the delightful music now being played by the Flyers' turnstiles as consolation. Sellouts were commonplace and, slowly but surely, hockey was becoming the hottest entertainment in town.

Now all Ed Snider needed was a winner.

15 / ... and More Heartbreak

Snider, the handsome, greying, onetime certified public accountant, took his setbacks as graciously as any rabid owner–fan might be expected to. Sure he wanted a winner, but in the meantime he was having great fun.

The departure of Bill Putnam consolidated Snider's power. And whether his enemies liked it or not, Ed Snider now was calling the shots for NHL hockey in Philadelphia.

"Snider's work day," said an acquaintance of his, "consists of 24 hours a day, seven days a week. When it comes to the Flyers, and it usually does, the man is nuts. This is unusual in professional sports. The owner is supposed to be the guy with the money who sits back in some big office and smokes hand-rolled cigars while he watches the bread roll in.

"He is not supposed to get involved with day-to-day matters. He is not supposed to get involved with the semi-educated, numbered mountains of muscle at the playing end of his payroll. He is not supposed to get his custom-made suits spoiled by the smell of the locker room after a good game. These are the unwritten rules of being an owner, and Ed Snider breaks every one of them."

129

One of many near-legendary Snider stories involves a vacation he was taking several seasons ago in Maine, theoretically to get away from it all. There was only one problem: this vacation was during the regular NHL campaign and Snider began thinking about his Flyers. The more he thought, the more he wanted information; except that he was secluded from telephones, radios, and other forms of communication.

"It was game night," wrote Maury Levy of *Philadelphia Magazine*, "and Snider just couldn't take it. He drove all the way down through the slush and traffic to get to the Spectrum in time to catch most of the last two periods."

Snider soon earned a reputation on the NHL's austere Board of Governors as the mod boss of hockey, a man whose progressive ideas not only had to be tolerated but merited serious consideration as well.

Snider's thinking was evident in his front office. Publicity man Joe Kadlec, one of the original Flyers, proved to be the most innovative and cooperative in the league. Lou Scheinfeld, a former *Philadelphia Daily News* reporter, moved rapidly up to a Flyers' vice presidency and became one of the best inside organization men in sports. Scheinfeld was credited with saving the Spectrum from being called Keystone Arena and the Flyers from being called the Quakers.

To beef up the radio-television operation, Snider imported Harlan Singer to produce and direct the team's broadcasts. And, of course, there was Marcel Pelletier, the player personnel director, to provide levity with his logic so that gloom never enshrouded the front office for very long.

From Snider to Scheinfeld to Kadlec to Pelletier the Philadelphia NHL operation was big-league all the way, but with one big question mark—coach Vic Stasiuk.

It wasn't that Stasiuk was a bad coach; he couldn't have been considering that he had practiced his thankless trade for eight years and, prior to that, had played 742 NHL games. The husky, galvanic Stasiuk certainly knew professional hockey. But he was a taskmaster.

"If it weren't for hockey," Maury Levy observed, "Stasiuk would be a deaf mute. Hockey is all he hears, all he talks about."

Unfortunately, few professional athletes are as dedicated to their sport as Vic Stasiuk and the Philadelphia team was no exception. The players bridled when he moved a soda pop machine out of the dressing room and they griped about his line-changes and assorted other edicts until dissension stories filled the newspapers.

"The unrest," said Bill Fleischman of *The Philadelphia Daily News*, "centered around Stasiuk's old-school ideas. In many respects there is nothing wrong with his ideas but many contemporary players snicker at the hockey-24-hours-a-day way of life."

A pragmatist from the drop of the puck, manager Allen was aware of the discontent and began his own personal probe after the brief Chicago playoff series. "I talked with some players," Allen confirmed, "and there was some static which isn't unusual. But the more I talked the more I saw there was an almost-unanimous undercurrent.

"I considered discussing all this with Vic and suggesting that he change, but I knew that that would be delaying the inevitable. We'd be sitting on a firecracker. There was no way Vic could change his rapport with this team."

On May 27, 1971, Stasiuk was fired. Snider asserted that the decision was Allen's which meant it was a more difficult move than usual since Allen genuinely liked Vic and had been a hard-line mentor himself. Yet Allen handled the explanation, citing player dissatisfaction as his reason for dropping the man he liked so much.

"I told Vic he's an idealist," said Allen. "Some guys don't want to be as good as Bobby Orr or Phil Esposito. They know they're good enough to play in the NHL and they're happy. Vic could never buy that."

The knowledge that hard, honest toil and a 110 percent effort was not enough to preserve his job—let alone a playoff berth—came as a shock to Stasiuk.

"It hit me pretty hard," recalls Vic. "You hate to have someone tell you you're no good as a coach. My stubbornness in not accepting a so-so effort got me in trouble. I've been told I have to change with the times and I can believe it. But I have to be shown my ways are wrong before I will believe it."

With Stasiuk out of the picture, Allen cast about for a suitable replacement. He understood that he needed a good one because now his job was on the line as well. Allen dipped into the New York Rangers' organization and plucked 46-year-old Fred Shero who, apparently, had been the long-range choice to succeed Emile Francis as coach in New York.

But Francis was not quite ready to relinquish his coaching reins and Shero was becoming impatient with the minors where he had developed a handsome dossier including the 1971 Central League championship with Omaha. When word got out that Shero had the job, hockey men lauded Allen for a brilliant catch. One of these was ex-Flyer, Reg Fleming, who recalled Shero as his minor-league mentor.

It was Fleming who first suggested that Shero would develop a "Mean Machine" in Philadelphia; just as Shero had done in the minor leagues as far back as the late Fifties when he coached the Shawinigan Falls Cataracts in the fast Quebec League.

"Shawinigan is where I became known as a fighter," said Fleming, "and Shero, who was my coach there, sort of egged me on to be more aggressive. He'd say 'Don't you worry about the fines. You just go out there and do your best, and if you have a fight, then fight!'

"Fred did as much as anyone to build up my confidence. I felt that he was a guy who really wanted to help me and, as a result, I did my best for him. And it finally paid off for us both. On top of that, Fred was a boxing enthusiast, and had once been a good boxer. He would take three or four of us in his car to see the fights whenever we could."

At his first Philadelphia press conference, Shero neither promised a Stanley Cup nor a Clarence Campbell Bowl. He spoke softly and when asked how he would compare his coaching with Stasiuk's, he replied: "I don't like to say whether I can do another man's job better than he can until I've done it. I've never coached in the big leagues before."

After neatly fielding a few banal questions, Shero zeroed in on the philosophy of his business. "The best team doesn't necessarily win. That's the reason you have coaches. If you had the best team, you wouldn't need a coach."

When someone asked Shero how high he could lift the Flyers, he mulled the question for a moment. "I don't think it's unreasonable to expect a second-place finish."

Nobody laughed out loud but several snickers were detected in the next day's newspapers. *Inquirer* columnist Frank Dolson was somewhat less than subtle when he asked:

"Wasn't Shero aware that he had just taken a giant step towards an early retirement? Didn't this gentle-looking, pleasant man know that he had just sentenced himself to three years of hard labor for Ed Snider, the Charlie Finley of the Atlantic Seaboard?"

The needles didn't disturb Shero because he too had a sense of humor, and Flyers' personnel director Marcel Pelletier swore to that by telling about the times he had played for Shero. Once in St. Paul Fred's team had a 7–1 lead with only a few minutes remaining. "The fans started leaving the place," Pelletier remembered. "They were bored."

Shero decided to shock them into staying. He pulled Pelletier out of the net and finished the game with six skaters and a gaping goal. "The final score," Shero recalled, "was 7–3."

Another time Shero's club was leading 5–0 with four minutes to go when, once again, Pelletier got the hook. "There were 6000 people in the stands," said Shero. "We were trying to give them a show. Well, we won 7–5, and they hit the post three times."

There would be no such tomfoolery in the NHL because it appeared doubtful that the Flyers would be capable of mounting a 5–0 lead. Shero, like his predecessor, had blueprinted a competitive club but one that hardly was capable of a second-place challenge. They settled into a three-way fight for the third and fourth spots with St. Louis and Pittsburgh, a battle that would carry right down to the final month and—in the case of the Flyers and Penguins—to the last game of the campaign.

Shero, who had been through the school of hard hockey knocks, explored new realms of disaster that seemed a Flyers' specialty as the 1971–72 season reached the homestretch. Tragedy, in its worst form, struck viciously at the embattled Philadelphians on a night in February 1972 during a game against the Canucks at Vancouver.

The coach had dispatched veteran Bruce Gamble to the nets for that encounter; and Gamble, who had played goal for 144 pro years in 11 hockey towns, played superbly. At 33, the blocky goalie who appeared to be all shoulders and barrel chest was never better. But though he beat Vancouver, 3–1, an incident during the game signalled the disaster.

One moment Gamble was standing in front of the pipes fending pucks, and the next moment he was lying on the ice. He tried to get up and couldn't. He tried again and, slowly, he made it.

Gamble turned to his defenseman Barry Ashbee and said, "Who hit me?"

"Who hit you?" Ashbee said, sort of frowning.

"Yeah, who hit me? Who knocked me down?"

"Jeez, Bruce, I don't know," Ashbee replied. "I didn't see anybody hit you."

The episode took place early in the game, yet Gamble remained in the nets to finish. "I don't think I've ever seen better goaltending," said manager Allen. "Bruce was so confident, so sure of himself. He was doing everything right."

Center Bobby Clarke echoed Allen's sentiments. "We can thank God for Bruce tonight. He saved us. If anyone in here prays, he should say a prayer for Bruce."

Ironically, neither Clarke nor Allen nor Gamble realized at the time that the goaltender had suffered a heart attack during the game. Gamble flew with the team to Oakland on a charter flight, but experienced discomfort during the evening and was taken to Merritt Hospital by assistant trainer Warren Elliott.

"At first," said Elliott, "we thought it was fatigue and maybe high blood pressure; but when Bruce complained of a tightening in the chest, I figured I'd better get him to a hospital for tests right away."

Dr. Joseph Clift examined Gamble and diagnosed the heart attack. He told Allen that Gamble was finished for the rest of the season. Bruce later would learn that he would never play NHL hockey again. On that night in Vancouver he lost his goaltending career and his dreams, at the age of 33.

When he recovered the Flyers appointed him a scout, but fate's cruel blow had left its sting. "We liked Philadelphia a lot," said Gamble once he was back on his feet again. "And I was finally making the money. I figured that for the next four, five years I'd be making forty thousand easy, maybe fifty. That'd do things for my pension."

Losing Gamble was a double-barreled blow to the Flyers. Bruce had a winning record and the Philadelphians were approaching the most important part of the schedule with the enigmatic Doug Favell as their No. 1 goaltender. Worse still, they didn't have Gamble as back-up.

Still the Flyers remained in playoff contention right down to the final night of the season when they played the Sabres at Buffalo. A win or a tie would mean fourth place even if their pursuers, the Pittsburgh Penguins, won their home game against St. Louis that night.

The Buffalo scoreboard began revealing grim news for the Flyers from Pittsburgh where the Penguins were skating to an easy 6–2 victory over the Blues. No matter. A tie would be just fine for Philadelphia and the Flyers had the situation well in hand.

Bobby Clarke put them ahead at 19:51 of the first period and Rick Foley made it 2–0 Philadelphia at 8:53 of the second. Favell, so far, had been impenetrable.

Buffalo, however, failed to play dead and less than two minutes later Gil Perreault broke free of the Flyers' defense, put two big feints on Favell and now the Flyers lead was cut to one. "We knew what we had to do," said Shero. "We were watching the scoreboard and saw what was happening in Pittsburgh."

Philadelphia escaped the second period still leading 2–1. In the last period the Sabres were manacled throughout the first eight minutes, but Ed Van Impe was tagged with a hooking penalty and on came the Sabres' power play. At 8:47 Rene Robert tied the score. The Flyers were now one goal away from blowing fourth place.

"Even after Buffalo tied us," Shero explained, "we were going for the victory. But in the last three or four minutes we started playing for the tie. I decided it would be better to make sure of getting into the playoffs. I told the team only one man was to go in deep and that the wings should pick up their men. We were doing the job . . ."

Tenaciously, the Flyers checked every Buffalo attempt to move the puck toward Favell until there were less than 50 seconds remaining in the period. Sabres' manager–coach Punch Imlach had two of his favorite skaters on the ice, Mike Byers and Gerry Meehan, both of whom had been with the Flyers.

"I looked up at the scoreboard," said Meehan, "and the message up there said I had once played 12 games with the

Flyers. I kept thinking 'Wouldn't it be funny if I scored the goal that made it 3–2?' "

Now with less than ten seconds remaining, the Flyers were preparing to vault the boards and embrace goalie Favell for the start of their playoff-clinching celebration. But then Byers trapped the puck in his end of the rink and spotted Meehan near the center red line. His pass was true and Meehan took it squarely on his stick in full flight toward the Philadelphia goal.

At the moment Meehan received the puck, defenseman Van Impe moved into position at the Flyers' blue line. "Van Impe was in front of me," Meehan recalled, "and he kept backing in. I think maybe he screened Favell a little. I just wound up and shot."

The puck orbited and sped on target toward the right side of the net as Meehan watched its dramatic flight about knee high. "I never saw it," said Favell, "until it was on top of me."

When he finally saw it, Favell frantically kicked out his left pad. "It went right past his knee," Meehan noted.

Favell collapsed to the ice, falling on his left buttock as the fateful puck stuck in the webbing of the net. "I couldn't believe it," said the forlorn goalie.

"Could you believe it," groaned defenseman Jean Potvin. "We lost fourth place with four seconds to go."

If anyone in Philadelphia suspected that it was nothing more than a nightmare, the headlines confirmed their worst fears. FOUR SECONDS AWAY AND WE DON'T MAKE IT, proclaimed *The Bulletin.*

The normally phlegmatic Shero, who had suggested a second-place finish and wound up fifth, nearly broke down in the silent Flyers' dressing room after the game. "I feel," Shero said, "the same way I did when my mother and father died."

16/

Fred Shero Takes Command

When Fred Shero was selected to replace Vic Stasiuk as Flyers' coach the displaced Stasiuk stunned interviewers with nothing but kind words for his successor.

"When I coached against Fred in the Central and American Leagues," said Stasiuk, "I could get mad at all the other coaches but never at Shero. And I don't know why. Maybe it's because he's just not controversial. He never gets in any arguments. You just can't get mad at the guy."

Well, nobody got terribly mad at Shero when the Flyers blew a playoff berth on the final night of the 1971–72 season; at least not mad enough to fire him. The front office sensed that Shero was too good a man to lose and they were particularly pleased with the way he tuned in to the younger players.

This was no accident. Having coached since 1957, Fred had studied the profession carefully. He was aware of the evolution, the changing balance of power from ownership to players as the demand for skaters exceeded the supply.

"In my playing days," Shero recalled, "mangement was in

complete control. Now players are rebelling over any little slight and protesting. But people are doing it in every part of the world; students, everybody.

"The way I feel, though, the coach's authority should be absolute. If a player has something to say, let it be said in the dressing room. Let it stay there if it can be thrashed out. But if it can't, then one of them has to quit. You can't have 18 players doing the coaching."

After one season it was apparent that the cool, calm, collected Shero was as different from the explosive Stasiuk as ice from fire.

"You know," Shero explained, "I've hardly ever fined a player. Money means nothing nowadays. You fine people and they laugh at you. But you sit him on the bench and it's embarrassing. Embarrassing to his family, to his teammates, to him. It's very hard for players to say when they should go out on the ice. But if I keep a player on the bench, I'll have a reason for it and we'll discuss it.

"I tell my guys: I don't want you to do what I say unless I can prove I'm right."

From June 1972 through June 1973 Shero made almost no significant mistakes, though he did make several vital innovative moves that would alter the entire perspective of the team. His first made at the beginning of this time, was an important as any, yet it became buried under the avalanche of hockey news then breaking across the sports pages.

The Flyers announced that Mike Nykoluk had been named assistant coach of the team. To Pennsylvania hockey fans the name Nykoluk was meaningful. Mike had been a crack right wing with the Hershey (Pa.) Bears of the American League since 1958 and earlier had been a star for the Toronto Marlboros when the junior team won the Memorial Cup of Canada in 1955.

In 17 seasons as a professional, Nykoluk totalled more than 700 assists and, as one observer put it, "Mike knows what offense is all about." Which was precisely why Shero hired him. The Flyers' defense was fine but the offense sputtered like a two cylinder engine.

"Nykoluk can solve that problem," said *Toronto Star* sports editor Jim Proudfoot. "The Flyers have come to realize that coaching can be improved by adding a specialist like Nykoluk. His appointment is an historic breakthrough."

Another historic breakthrough was also providing the Flyers with ulcers. The World Hockey Association had come into being and, among other things, revealed that it would place a team in Philadelphia—the Blazers. Meanwhile, New York's WHA team, the Raiders, had made it clear that they were bent on signing Bill Flett, Brent Hughes, and Dave Schultz of the Flyers and even went so far as to invite the players to a press conference at the Statler-Hilton Hotel in New York to introduce them to the media.

There was little that Ed Snider and Company could do about the Blazers except hope they would go away. But they didn't. Each week brought smashing news about the new WHA club in Philadelphia. They signed popular Boston Bruins wing Johnny McKenzie as player–coach. They captured outstanding young defenseman Ron Plumb from the Boston organization by offering him a staggering salary and, one by one, they began luring other NHL skaters into their fold.

But the biggest coup was yet to come. After a long series of negotiations between Blazers president Jim Cooper and

Boston sports attorney Bob Woolf, the team signed controversial center Derek Sanderson to a multi-million dollar contract amid fuss and fanfare in center Philadelphia. Suddenly the Blazers had a celebrity to compete with the Flyers' Bobby Clarke.

Snider conceded Sanderson to the WHA; there was little he could do about that. But there was something he could do about the Flyers being wooed by the New York Raiders. He could get them back. Which is precisely what Snider did. And while the Raiders were jubilantly telling their prospective customers that Flett, Hughes, and Schultz would lead New York to a WHA crown, the trio put their signatures to Flyers' contracts and all was right with the world once again at the Spectrum.

It was the last time the WHA posed a threat to the Flyers' dominance of the Philadelphia hockey territory.

With the tempestuous Schultz in the fold, Shero realized that he now had the makings of an extremely tough hockey club. Tough and big. Schultz 6'1", 185; Don Saleski, 6'2", 198; Gary Dornhoefer, 6'2", 185; Ross Lonsberry, 5'10", 190; Bob Kelly, 5'11", 198; Rick MacLeish, 5'11", 185; not to mention a herd of bull-like defensemen orchestrated by one of the originals, Ed Van Impe.

It was a far cry from the Flyer team which had once been chased out of the playoffs by St. Louis.

"We were intimidated in those days," asserted Snider, "and I said to myself that it would never happen to a club of mine again."

And so the magnificent Mean Machine was born and sent out to terrorize the NHL in 1972–73, and maybe even win a playoff berth.

17/

The Magnificent Mean Machine

CAN THE FLYERS' MEAN MACHINE CRUNCH THIS BUNCH? The question sat atop an NHL schedule distributed throughout Philadelphia to hockey fans interested in purchasing season tickets. "This Bunch" happened to be the 15 other NHL teams who, during the next seven months, had the misfortune of getting in the Flyers' way.

Some victims did better than others. The big bad Boston Bruins, for example, were hardly bruised but when they left the Spectrum they knew they had been in a hockey game. By contrast, the Vancouver Canucks were crushed like a saltine under a mallet. The others were blacked and blued and—in the case of Detroit—screamed bloody murder, demanding that the Broad Street Bullies be punished by NHL President Clarence Campbell.

For sure, nobody scared the Flyers anymore; not even Boston. "In other years," said Bobby Clarke, "we'd play the

Bruins in Boston and figure they had a two-goal lead to start with. Now it's even."

Only one figure frightened the Flyers and that was the black-and-white striped referee who, as the 1972–73 season progressed, began to take greater and greater note of the ferocious Flyers.

So did the strong teams of the NHL, although several required a rude awakening during the early months of the 1972–73 season. The regal Montreal Canadiens were just such a one. On the night of December 3, 1972, the Canadiens invaded the Spectrum and, instead of starting their first-string goalie, Ken Dryden, Montreal coach Scotty Bowman called on the inexperienced and little-used Michel Plasse.

Suitably provoked, the angry Flyers nearly ran the Montrealers out of the rink and stung the visitors with a 5–2 defeat. Still fuming even *after* the victory, Bobby Clarke betrayed the team's new pride by singling out coach Bowman for unusual criticism.

"Hasn't he (Bowman) got any respect for the Flyers?" snapped Clarke. "What's he doin' with the best goalie in the league sitting in the press box? When we saw Dryden wasn't dressed for the game a lot of us were teed off."

The more teed off the Flyers became the better, it seems they played. By the end of 1972, they not only had established themselves as first-rate contenders in the West Division but also as the holy terrors of the league. The reputation resulted from a series of Pier Six brawls, smaller skirmishes and a not-very-subtle assertion by the front office that Fred Shero's sextet would be delighted to beat up on anybody in sight.

One game more than any other underlined the ferociousness of the new Flyers, and from that point (December 29, 1972) on the Magnificent Mean Machine became the most fearsome thing on ice since the big bad Bruins of 1969.

The incendiary event took place at Vancouver's Pacific Coliseum during the third period of a 4–4 tie. According to Vancouverites, the first and most disturbing act of provocation was supplied by Flyers' rookie Don Saleski who was beating up Barry Wilcox of the Canucks.

Saleski was doing such a destructive job on Wilcox that a Vancouver fan felt obliged to intervene on behalf of the local skater. The spectator reached over the boards and grabbed a handful of Saleski's abundant hairs.

"I thought he was going to pull me right off the ice," said Saleski, amazed.

The spectator made the mistake of perpetrating this act near the Flyers' bench. Immediately, the Philadelphians charged over the boards and engaged a flock of the loyal in combat. Sticks flew, heads ducked, and the police charged on to the scene. One gendarme, Corporal Donald Brown, attempted to pull the Flyers' spare goalie, Bob Taylor, away from the melee, but the officer himself wound up on the ground. The Vancouver spectators charged that the Flyers acted like animals while Philadelphia coach Shero claimed there would have been no trouble if the authorities had heeded his warning.

"There were no cops in the runway at all," Shero protested, "and I had requested some. The people were hollering and throwing things in the first period and I expected trouble. I told an usher but he did nothing. Our law and order on the ice is maintained by a referee. If the fans reach out there and get involved they deserve what they get. This is as old as hockey itself."

The episode took place while NHL President Clarence Campbell was hospitalized for gall bladder tests in Montreal. His deputy, vice president Don Ruck, studied the game reports and issued what amounted to a mild slap-on-the-wrist to the belligerents.

"Under heavy provocation from fans," said Ruck, "a hockey player will react like any other human being. Analyzing something like this is like trying to crawl into somebody's mind. Some people have shorter fuses than others. What do you do when a lady spills coffee in your lap? Say thank you or punch her in the nose?

"It's unfortunate that fans can't remain in the area they purchased—and that's the same as the width of their butt."

Whatever the rationale, Philadelphia jumped to the top of the visiting team hate parade in Vancouver. Soon they'd be on top in Detroit, Buffalo, and Montreal as well. "The Flyers," said Chuck Newman of *The Inquirer*, "have earned the dislike of fans and officials throughout the league."

"Maybe we ought to lay low for a while," suggested Bill Flett.

To which rookie Bill Barber replied: "The referees will have to change. They can't make us change our style."

There certainly was no change in the Flyers' style on February 9, 1973, when they returned to Vancouver to defeat the Canucks 10–5 and tighten their grip on second place. They clobbered the club at every opportunity.

PHILLY BULLIES PACK MEAN PUNCH, declared a headline in *The Vancouver Sun*. And "Villainous" was the adjective used by *Sun* reporter Arv Olson to describe the Philadelphia team.

Andre Dupont of the Flyers clipped Bobby Schmautz of Vancouver on the forehead with his stick. Dave Schultz belted Schmautz in a fight. And later Schultz took on Dale Tallon of the Canucks. Tallon retired from the game with a seven-stitch cut over his eye and a pulled stomach muscle. These were just a few of the bouts.

Guerrilla warfare such as this caught the fancy of hockey fans across the continent. They regarded the Flyers as a throw-back to the pioneering days of the game when brawls were a dime-a-dozen and nobody thought twice about it. National magazines began zeroing in on Shero's warriors and, of course, the more puritanical element grabbed their typewriters and condemned the Broad Street Bullies for defacing hockey's good name. Columnist Jim Taylor of *The Vancouver Sun* was especially furious.

"If the NHL wants to condone goon squads like the Flyers," said Taylor, "if the Canucks are silly enough to play along and the customers are suckers enough to buy it, who am I to say no? There's just one thing that bothers me. The Flyers play butcher shop hockey and succeed by the only measuring stick that counts. They win.

"Success breeds imitators. If they make it to the Stanley Cup final, how many more goon squads can we expect next season?"

Taylor wasn't the only dissenter. Some critics argued that it was easy to play bully-boy against a lighthorse team like the Canucks. But how rough would the Flyers be against some of the bigger NHL clubs? A few members of the Pittsburgh Penguins inferred that the Flyers were Filthy McNastys on their home Broad Street rink but were more lamblike on the road. The Penguins then made the mistake of inciting the Flyers to disprove that theory on January 27 at Pittsburgh's Civic Arena. The result was a Philadelphia club record of 80 penalty minutes, a silenced Penguins' team, and a bruised referee Bryan Lewis who walked into defenseman Barry Ashbee's opened-handed punch. Not so coincidentally, the Flyers won the game 5–3, breaking a four-and-a-half-year Civic Arena jinx.

Once again, the Flyers took decision after decision. In one confrontation, defenseman Andre "Moose" Dupont mauled Jean-Guy Legace of Pittsburgh. When Dupont heard that Legace received a five-minute major penalty, he couldn't help chuckling.

"Legace," commented Dupont, "should have gotten five minutes for receiving, not fighting."

Such a swaggering attitude did nothing to endear the Flyers to the opposition, which was precisely the style of the Mean Machine. Intimidation was the key word. If the enemy didn't like it, well, the Philadelphians simply paraphrased the Emperor Caligula: *"Oderint dum metuant."* (Let them hate us as long as they fear us.)

"The intimidation hasn't hurt us," said Shero. "Fights are okay because we take another guy off with us. I like to think we're winning on finesse, but it's good to soften 'em up first."

Former NHL badman Bobby Baun once remarked that no player in the NHL can win every fight he's in and that eventually somebody comes along to give a beating to the fellow who thinks he's the toughest man on ice. The law of averages finally caught up with Dave Schultz on February 17, 1973, at the Forum in Montreal.

Schultz detonated the first explosion early in the game when he tossed a left hook at Guy Lafleur, an especially clean player, and then wrestled with smallish Canadien captain Henri Richard. Late in the first period Schultz made the mistake of charging big Montreal defenseman Serge Savard. With a flurry of crisp punches, Savard floored Schultz and when the Flyer got back to his feet Pierre Bouchard of the Canadiens walloped him again.

If that wasn't sufficient punishment for Schultz, Montreal coach Scotty Bowman then asked referee Lloyd Gilmour to measure Dave's stick. Gilmour discovered that Schultz's stick blade was illegal and hit him with a minor penalty as well as the two majors for fighting. But the Flyers still won the game 7–6 with less than four minutes remaining.

Beating the Canucks in Vancouver was little enough. But when the Flyers stormed the Forum and defeated Montreal, everyone from New York to Los Angeles took notice.

"After five years of arriving at rival arenas to the accompaniment of yawns," wrote Bill Fleischman in *The Philadelphia Daily News*, "the Flyers are now a genuine attraction. At nearly every NHL stop, people ask: 'Are these guys really that tough?' Then, people go out and boo the Mad Squad."

The boos never were more intense than at Detroit's Olympia Stadium where the Flyers infuriated the Red Wings' fans on the night of February 28, 1973, in a game that produced four major battles and 134 record-breaking penalty minutes. Then Detroit coach, Johnny Wilson, blew his cool completely after the game although his club had eked out a 6–5 win. As far as Wilson was concerned, the Flyers should have been banished to the Arctic Circle, for all the good they were doing hockey.

"Something should be done about this," demanded the irate Wilson. "They're letting brutality get in the game. They have a lawsuit against them. No team will back down, man-to-man, but all that holding, hooking, and spearing doesn't make sense. You don't win hockey games playing like animals."

Except that the Flyers were challenging for first place while the Red Wings were losing out in their battle to reach a playoff berth.

Fearsome and sinister on the ice, the Mean Machine was a collection of happy players away from the rink. They were, of course, sprinkled with French-Canadians but cliques—the bane of a bilingual hockey club—never seemed to develop. And when soothing spirits were needed, assistant coach Mike Nykoluk always managed to be handy to cope with the problem.

One of Nykoluk's innovations was a regular "Breakfast with Mike" ritual where he would sit down with players who, for one reason or another, might need some special attention at the time.

"It's not a bad idea," admitted Don Saleski with a wide grin, "but it would be better at 10 A.M. Having it at 8 A.M. *really* makes it breakfast!"

The Flyers' shake, rattle, and roll philosophy was not quite enough to lift them over the Chicago Black Hawks and into first place in the West Division; but on March 31, 1973, the next to last night of the regular schedule, Philadelphia did clinch second with a 10–2 mauling of the New York Islanders.

On the final night, the Flyers lost 5–4 at Pittsburgh as Rick MacLeish became only the eighth man in NHL history to score 50 goals.

To the question raised at the start of the long campaign—CAN THE FLYERS' MEAN MACHINE CRUNCH THIS BUNCH?—the answer was in the affirmative. Philadelphia had proven once again the validity of a remark made decades ago by former Toronto Maple Leafs' manager Conn Smythe: "If you can beat 'em in the alley, you can beat 'em on the ice."

18/

But We Can Play Hockey Too

Even in 1968, the year the Flyers won the Clarence Campbell Bowl, Philadelphia was wiped out of the playoffs in the first round.

In that series, against St. Louis, it took seven games. A year later the Blues shellacked them in a humbling four straight and the Chicago Black Hawks were equally punishing in 1971.

It clearly was time for a change and the Magnificent Mean Machine would have its mettle tested in the opening round of the 1973 playoffs by Minnesota's veteran North Stars.

While the North Stars had finished behind the Flyers during the regular schedule, coach Jack Gordon's club was respected for its experience, its disciplined style of play, and the competent goaltending of lean, long Cesare Maniago.

Flyers' coach Shero named erratic Doug Favell to go against Maniago in the Cup opener at the Spectrum. "As long as Doug plays well," Shero explained, "he stays in there. As for the rest of the guys; they had better not take too many foolish penalties against Minnesota. The North Stars are smart. They have a good power play and they have the experience that we don't."

Observers questioned Philadelphia's ability to carry their *blitzkrieg* to advantage in the more diligently officiated playoffs. Others pointed out that Minnesota had a Mean Machine of their own with such blasters as Dennis Hextall, Ted Harris, Dennis O'Brien, and Tom Reid.

The Flyers failed their first test with terrible grades. They lost the game, 3–0, before more than 16,000 disillusioned fans and they hardly intimidated the visitors, although Dave Schultz desperately tried to antagonize Hextall, who led the North Stars in points and penalties.

"I didn't want to spend five minutes in the penalty box," Hextall explained with a derisive leer, "not with a 20-point man like Schultz."

Schultz, who had been outscored by Hextall 82–21 on the season, spent considerable time needling the North Stars' ace but Dennis, the Minnesota menace, saved his barbs for the dressing room after the victory.

"So far," twitted Hextall, "Schultz still has to prove himself to me. Fights take a lot out of you. It hurts my team when I'm off the ice."

Meanwhile, at the other end of the corridor, Coach Shero diagnosed the Flyers' faux pas. "The kids," he said with a frown, "acted more like veterans and my veterans played the way you'd expect rookies to play. I couldn't understand what was happening."

Shero was disturbed but not discouraged. He had been around too many playoffs to believe that the series was over with the first loss. "The playoffs," he stated, "remind me of a heavyweight championship fight. You know how the fighters come out and maybe feel each other out for three, four rounds. Then, once you're over the jitters and have the other guy figured, then, whammo, may the best man win. Same with the playoffs. By the third or fourth game, you'll see some real hockey. The best team will prevail."

As usual, Shero was on the right track. Staggered though they were by the opener, the Flyers counterattacked in the second Spectrum match to win, 4–1. The North Stars took the third game, 5–0, played at Bloomington, Minnesota. Now the real hockey was underway.

The Flyers won the fourth game 3–0, and the series was tied at two apiece. The remaining contests would separate the men from the boys and determine, once and for all, whether the Mean Machine was simply punches, elbows, and butt ends.

"I look for power plays to be very important from now on," said Van Impe. "Some of these guys are due to break loose."

In what developed as the pivotal game of the series at the Spectrum, Philadelphia won Game Five on Gary Dornhoefer's goal at 8:35 of sudden death overtime. The sixth game was scheduled for the Metropolitan Sports Center in Bloomington on April 12, 1973. An historic occasion for the Flyers.

Shero's choice in goal, as it had been throughout the series, was 28-year-old Favell who remained an enigmatic figure to the coach and many Flyers' fans. Favell was like the little girl with the curl: when he was good he was very, very good and when he was bad he was horrid.

Midway through the 1972–73 season Shero publicly criticized Favell for the goalie's uninspired behavior during practice sessions. At one point in the schedule Shero betrayed his displeasure by benching Favell in favor of the less-experienced Michel Belhumeur and Bob Taylor.

So disturbed by the benching was Favell, he once asked reporters: "What am I, a head of lettuce?"

But Shero knew what side his lettuce was buttered on; and so when it came to the vital homestretch games, he beckoned to Doug who came through nobly. Likewise, Shero wanted Favell to remain in the nets throughout the Minnesota series—if Favell could handle the pressure and the fatigue.

"I'm tired physically," Favell admitted before the sixth game, "but I'm ready."

Though Favell may have been tired, the North Stars were demoralized by the Philadelphia goaltender. His performances were clearly more than the Minnesotans had bargained for, especially coach Jack Gordon.

"I was already counting a couple of those goals Favell made stops on in the earlier games," said Gordon. "If a few had gone in, it would have been a different series."

But could dauntless Doug extend his miraculous goaltending one more game? The answer came during the first period at Minnesota on April 12, 1973. Favell allowed but one goal, though the North Stars had swarmed around his cage all period and outshot the Flyers 13–4. Holding the Minnesota sextet to one goal under these circumstances gave Shero's skaters the lift they needed while resting between periods.

After Terry Crisp tied the score, Favell spectacularly stopped Dean Prentice of Minnesota, and suddenly the tide turned for the Flyers. Ross Lonsberry then drifted over the blue line and flicked an unusually soft shot at Maniago that somehow fooled him. "The puck looked like a monarch butterfly," said Lonsberry. "I sure didn't get much on it, but they don't ask how you scored, just how many."

Less than two minutes later Dave Schultz was smashed to the ice by defenseman Ted Harris. He considered charging back at the North Star but had second thoughts and lifted himself back to the action just in time to nab Bobby Clarke's pass. Schultz slid the puck under Maniago to give Philadelphia a 3–1 lead.

"I'm glad I fell right away when Harris hit me," Schultz recalled, "otherwise I might have gone after him and not been in position for Bobby's pass."

Fortified with a two-goal lead, the Flyers' defense of Ed Van Impe, Joe Watson, Barry Ashbee, and Andre Dupont proved unbeatable as the North Stars were stopped cold at the Philadelphia blue line.

"The Flyers' defense," observed Gordon, "was very sound."

Minnesota never scored again. In the final minute Gordon desperately yanked Maniago, but Lonsberry stole the puck and, with Dennis O'Brien between himself and the goal, hoisted it over the defenseman's head for the fourth and final score. "It was," said Rick MacLeish, "an 80-foot jump shot."

Philadelphia newsmen, who had been so harsh on the Flyers in the past, agreed that the defeat of the North Stars was a milestone in the team's young life. Both Bill Fleischman of the *Daily News* and Chuck Newman of *The Inquirer* called it "the greatest moment in Philadelphia hockey history."

Rookie Don Saleski symbolized the growth of this rambunctious group of athletes who had been scorned early in the season. "You're playing like a pro," a well-wisher said in the jubilant Philadelphia dressing room.

Saleski looked up at his friend and smiled the smile of confidence. "I am one now."

Unfortunately, the Flyers barely had time to savor their biggest triumph. In two days they were to meet the mighty Montreal Canadiens, champions of the East Division, in the first game of the semi-finals at Montreal.

Could Philadelphia topple so majestic a club as the vaunted Flying Frenchmen? Few experts thought so, least of all those in Montreal.

"There's no way Philadelphia can keep up with the Canadiens," stated writer Doug Gilbert of the Montreal *Gazette*. "But by carrying their elbows high all night and running everyone who goes in the corners into the boards, they sometimes can have the Canadiens dumping the puck in from afar and shooting from 50 feet out."

This was precisely what Shero had in mind as he planned his strategy. "There's no doubt," said the Flyers' coach, "that few teams can skate with the Canadiens. But there are things we can do to compensate for their speed. And there's no way we can play Montreal without having a real brawl somewhere along the line."

Shero's hope was to contain the Canadiens in their own territory before they could rev up their engines and outspeed his slower forwards. His problem was keeping his club "up" for the series after their devastation of the North Stars. "I'm worried," Shero explained, "that the players might think they have done their job by getting this far. We haven't won anything yet, except some money."

The Flyers never did win the Stanley Cup, but from the

opening faceoff against the Canadiens on April 14, 1973, until the moment of their exit from the semi-finals Philadelphia's exhuberant hockey team won a lot of respect from the sports world. And they began gathering kudos in that very game.

Back and forth, they traded goals with the Montrealers as the Forum fans marvelled at the manner in which the Flyers remained in the game. At the end of the regulation 60 minutes the score was tied, 4–4. What's more, the Flyers had stayed in the game without resorting to their usual bully-boy tactics. "You can't get tough," said Shero, "if the other team doesn't want to."

For two minutes of the sudden death overtime neither team scored. Then the Flyers sent the puck into the Canadiens' zone where the redoubtable All-Star left wing Frank Mahovlich took control. The man they call "Big M" then startled both his teammates and the Flyers with a maneuver that, years ago, was called the "Syracuse Pass" because any Toronto Maple Leaf player who used it was on the next train to the club's farm in Syracuse.

Mahovlich, an old pro who seldom indulged in such risky practices, passed the puck behind his back approximately 15 feet in front of his goalie, Ken Dryden. "He turned around to backhand a pass to one of his defensemen," remembered Rick MacLeish. "But the puck came right out to me."

MacLeish, who was fast developing into one of the game's outstanding opportunists, snatched the rubber from "a puddle of water" and flung it past the stunned and unprepared Dryden into the upper right corner of the net.

The Flyers were as incredulous as the 16,929 onlookers. "Why," said Lonsberry who was on the ice at the time, "I was turning up ice. I knew that Mahovlich never gives up the puck."

But through some quirk of fortune, Big M did commit the "Syracuse Pass" and now the Flyers began to believe that if that could happen why couldn't they march on to beat the Montrealers. A Philadelphia victory in the second game at the Forum would go a long way to assure them that a total playoff triumph was, after all, possible.

For three periods and six minutes of a sudden death overtime on April 17, 1973, the Flyers gave the Canadiens an awful scare. Philadelphia actually led the game, 3–2, until 11:50 of the third period when Yvan Cournoyer tied the score; but the Flyers took the initiative in the fateful extra period. "We were the stronger team in overtime," Flyer forward Simon Nolet noted. "We put on the most pressure."

They did except goalie Ken Dryden was having one of his better periods and the frustrated Flyers were kept off the scoresheet. The Forum clock showed six-and-a-half minutes gone by in overtime when Canadiens' rookie defenseman Larry Robinson put on a surprise burst of speed along the boards, fooling Gary Dornhoefer. Once over the Philadelphia blue line, Robinson released a 55-foot shot that baffled Favell and flew into the net at 6:45. Montreal had won 4–3 to tie the series at one apiece.

This was a bitter pill for the Flyers; doubly so because Montreal coach Scotty Bowman had become the *bête noire* of Philadelphia's skaters. What the Flyers displayed in muscle, Bowman seemed to be trying to offer in verbiage and he needled Dornhoefer relentlessly for missing Robinson on the game's decisive play.

"Robinson went around Dornhoefer right in front of our bench," sniped Bowman, "and Gary just waved at him."

Bowman's needle penetrated the Flyers sensitivities. Dornhoefer was the first to react when advised of Scotty's barbs. "He must be uptight," said Gary, "because we're going to cost him his job in this series."

Other Flyers pointed out that shots by Bill Flett and Don Saleski had beaten Dryden but hit the goalpost and bounced out of danger. Philadelphia skaters insisted that they would have won the game if either had gone in; but once again Bowman appeared unimpressed. "The goalpost," said Scotty, "is part of the equipment."

Yet the Flyers had a right to be proud of themselves. They went up to the Forum distinct underdogs and came away even in games and goals.

"We're going home now," said Shero. "That's a good feeling. My biggest fear is that we'll make a stupid play and the Philadelphia fans will get on us."

Bulletin columnist Jim Barniak was amused by Shero's problem and immediately put Shero and Flyers' fans on notice. "Are you kidding, Fred?" wrote Barniak. "The Flyers are all we've got. Anybody who boos a Flyer from here on out should get deported to the Arctic Circle."

In the Montreal camp, Canadien-watchers were wondering whether Bowman's boys would be able to sustain their winning way before an overwhelmingly hostile Spectrum crowd on April 19, 1973. A hint was dropped by Montreal captain Henri Richard who scoffed at the effectiveness of the Mean Machine.

"Who is this Schultz fellow?" asked Richard, tongue well-ensconced in cheek. "What's he ever done? A rookie. Same with Saleski. Big, tall guy, 6–3, a rookie, too. What's there to be worried about? Kelly, 'Bulldog' or whatever they call him. That's all."

Like Muhammad Ali once did, and then Bobby Riggs, Richard put his shots where his mouth is and the Canadiens showed the 16,000 Spectrum faithful why they are champions. Henri scored the winning goal in a 2–1 decision for the visitors despite an exciting last-ditch flurry by the Flyers.

"We're not discouraged," said Barry Ashbee. "Remember, we were down against Minnesota and came back."

But every last player knew the difference between the North Stars and the Canadiens. The Flyers simply could not win at home where they had to—they lost the fourth game— and returned to Montreal for what amounted to their 99th game of the season, counting exhibitions and the last gasp in their crusade for the Cup.

To their everlasting credit, Philadelphia didn't go out without raising a major fuss. They summoned what energy was left in their aching bodies—half the roster was injured in one way or another—and actually pulled ahead of the Canadiens, 3–2, at 5:30 of the third period.

Then, the "Montreal Mystique" overwhelmed the weary Philadelphians. Frank Mahovlich tied the score only 16 seconds later on a 65-foot shot that dipped under Doug Favell's glove and then Henri Richard again displayed his militant leadership by scoring the winning goal at 12:07. Yvan Cournoyer's tally moments later simply confirmed what every one of the 17,141 witnesses already knew: the Flyers were dead.

"At that point," recalled Bobby Clarke, "the body just wouldn't do what I wanted it to do."

Beaten but not unbowed the Flyers returned home. They had become hockey heros in Philadelphia like no other ice team the town had ever known. "The best," said Bowman, "comes out in a team when it's facing elimination. The Flyers were tough in the last game. They have nothing to be ashamed of."

They were greeted like heroes although they were not the victors. "They were disappointed," said their manager Allen, "but they knew in their hearts that they had given it their best shot. Three or four players told me they couldn't wait for next season. It means they're happy to be with our hockey club.

"These players know we've got something going, and we are going to get better."

III

The Ferocious Flyers

19/

Rick MacLeish,
the 50-Goal Scorer

It may be a bit hard to believe now, but the Flyers did not acquire Rick MacLeish from the Boston Bruins at the point of a gun. They simply sent their goalie, Bernie Parent, to the Toronto Maple Leafs, who sent their left winger, Mike Walton, to the Boston Bruins, who dispatched MacLeish to Philadelphia.

That was on February 1, 1970. Three years later MacLeish was on his way to a 50-goal season. In between there were some hard times—for MacLeish, for the Philadelphia brass, and especially for a Flyers' scout by the name of Les Moore.

On the day of the big trade Moore went out on a limb. "MacLeish," he said, "will score 15 goals between now and the end of the season." MacLeish came up 13 goals short of Moore's prediction. Then, in the first 17 games of the 1971–72 campaign, MacLeish managed just one goal for the Flyers. The next thing he knew he was toiling for Richmond in the American Hockey League.

Somewhere along the way scout Moore and the Flyers parted company. Whether the Flyers ever thought of giving up on MacLeish is one of those tantalizing questions that will never be answered. At the time of MacLeish's demotion to Richmond, however, general manager Keith Allen gave every indication that the Flyers were prepared to wait quite a long time for Rick to fulfill his potential.

"We haven't given up on the guy," Allen noted at the time. "He needs work and he wasn't getting it. In a way, I think he has been a victim of his own success in junior hockey. He was so good he didn't have to bear down his final year."

And, in fact, MacLeish was one of the sensations of the Ontario Hockey Association. That last year, with Peterborough, he had 45 goals and 56 assists in 54 games. He was the fourth player chosen in the year's amateur draft—by the Bruins—and he spent his first season as a professional with Oklahoma City of the Central League.

At that time the Bruins considered MacLeish to be the best forward in their farm system. But it was a case of unrequited love.

"I didn't learn a thing in Oklahoma City," MacLeish has said. "The coach (Murray Davidson) never told me anything. All he had us do was skate and do line rushes in practice."

MacLeish also was playing at wing instead of at center, which was his normal position. "I don't want to knock anybody," he says, "but my centerman wasn't the greatest and I never got on the ice on a power play."

Whatever the reason, or reasons, MacLeish had scored just 13 goals in 46 games with Oklahoma City when the Bruins, in effect, decided to sacrifice future possibilities for instant help in the form of an established NHL player, Mike Walton.

The Flyers, on the other hand, weren't under pressure to win the Stanley Cup immediately. Thus, Allen was able to say of the trade: "We dealt for youth and we're willing to wait for the kids to develop." But then he added, perhaps somewhat ominously: "Going to Richmond is MacLeish's big test. It will prove whether or not he has the desire to play in the NHL." It turned out that he did.

In 42 games with Richmond MacLeish netted 24 goals. But more than that he showed a willingness to play defensive as well as offensive hockey. He hit people. And he tried to excel in every phase of the game.

MacLeish also had matured enough to realize that while the Flyers were willing to be patient, they would not wait indefinitely for him to become a major leaguer. "I'm sure they were disappointed," MacLeish admits.

So disappointed, in fact, that at the start of training camp last season coach Fred Shero's big hope for stardom was another young center, Bill Clement. Once the season started, however, MacLeish made the Flyers and their fans forget not only Bill Clement, but just about every other player in the NHL.

Centering for the veteran Gary Dornhoefer and rookie Bill Barber, MacLeish scored 17 goals in Philadelphia's first 29 games.

"He can skate, pass, and shoot," Dornhoefer says. "He also works hard as hell."

By season's end MacLeish had 50 goals, making him—at 21—the youngest player in NHL history to reach that magic figure, and he also had 50 assists. That was just four points fewer than the total chalked up by Philadelphia's other out-standing center, Bobby Clarke, who was the NHL's Most Valuable Player.

"I've seen a lot of good hockey players, but I've never seen anyone as loose as Ricky," Clarke says in tribute to his team-mate. "They just can't get the puck away from him."

MacLeish, in the true Flyer tradition, is tough. Once, in junior hockey, he had a fight with Bob Kelly, now a team-mate.

"MacLeish just stood there and slugged it out with me," Kelly recalls. "I can honestly say I never lost a fight in junior, but that's one I didn't win."

A solid 5'11", 185 pounds, MacLeish says he has a similar record. "In the Central League I had seven fights and never lost one."

Beyond his fighting ability, however, MacLeish also has shown that he is "willing to play hurt." Early last season, for example, he suffered an ankle injury in a game against the Pittsburgh Penguins. It was painful, but he insisted on play-ing the next night, against the Black Hawks.

"MacLeish shook off that ankle injury very well," Shero explains, in recalling the incident. "But against the Hawks he got rapped on the head by a stick and the doctor told me not to play him after the first period.

"But he was doing everything for us, including winning faceoffs. I guess he plays okay when he's dizzy."

MacLeish also notched three goals that night as the Flyers beat the Hawks, 5–3.

Around Christmas 1972 MacLeish contracted tonsilitis. He never did shake the infection, but continued to play nonethe-less.

In the opening game of the 1973 Stanley Cup semi-final against Montreal, MacLeish scored the winning goal in a 5–4 victory at 2:56 of the first overtime. But he missed the next two games because of a 101-degree fever, and even when he did come back he just was too physically drained to be of much help to the Flyers. Had MacLeish been well, the outcome of the Philadelphia–Montreal series might have been different.

Even so, it was a highly successful season for the Flyers. And for MacLeish it was the season he became a star.

"It's just a matter of confidence," MacLeish says in explaining his sudden success. "Now that I've got something— a place on the team—I'm working harder."

Dornhoefer agrees that MacLeish is working harder . . . that he has one of the best wrist shots in the NHL . . . and that he has matured. But Gary also points out that MacLeish entered the NHL under a handicap.

"Those big buildups aren't good for anybody because they're hard to live up to—unless, of course, you're a Bobby Orr," Dornhoefer says. "It just means so much additional pressure."

Shero believes that MacLeish has conquered the pressure. Or, at least, he hopes he has.

"I think the only thing that could stop him is himself," Shero says. "He's got to give. If he does, there's no way he's not going to be a superstar.

"Right now, he's Mr. Everything," Shero continues. "I look for him to get more points in the future. He's got all the qualities necessary for greatness."

20/

Ed Van Impe,
Made by the Minors

In this day of goal-scoring defensemen, Ed Van Impe is a throwback to a long-gone era. The husky, heavily bearded veteran would rather prevent a score than flash the red light himself. He is also a rarity because of his lengthy and often painful education in hockey's minor leagues.

A native of Saskatoon, Saskatchewan, Van Impe began playing organized hockey at the age of six. His idol was the then great Doug Harvey of the Montreal Canadiens. "Harvey's style really impressed me," says Van Impe. "He always seemed to know what to do with the puck when he got it."

After three years of junior hockey in Saskatoon Ed was invited to the St. Catherines, Ontario, training camp of the Chicago Black Hawks. "I didn't know what to expect from the pros," he said. "It was pretty strange to be in the middle of stars like Glenn Hall, Bobby Hull, and Stan Mikita." His reward was a ticket to the Black Hawks' farm team in Calgary, Alberta, where he enjoyed a successful, albeit penalty-filled, season.

Despite his hopes of playing for the Black Hawks his second pro season, Van Impe was back in the minors again, this time at Buffalo. "I didn't realize it at the time," he said, "but I was going to be with Buffalo for five long years. Getting to the top was a slow, agonizing process but I learned all along the way."

Like many American Leaguers, Van Impe had his run-ins with Eddie Shore, then owner of the Springfield Indians, and a man notorious for his cavalier treatment of players. Once, he was drafted by Toronto and was supposed to report to Springfield, where Shore ruled as all-everything. After being briefly suspended for not reporting, Van Impe was traded back to Buffalo. "I just couldn't believe some of the things Shore did," Ed declared. He then recounted two of his favorite Shore tales. "One time our Buffalo club came in to play the Indians in Springfield. Before the game we were going through the usual warm-up, tossing shots at our goalie.

"We were given two pucks for the workout, but both of them had been deflected into the stands, so we needed another one. Shore had a habit of keeping the pucks in a bucket of ice water so they'd move easily over the surface during the game. He kept them right near the Springfield bench, a few feet away from his private box.

"When we had lost our last puck, I skated over to the pail to get a replacement, and Shore saw me coming. He ran down from his box and, just as I put my hand in the pail, he stuck his foot right into the pail—with his shoe on. His whole foot was soaking wet. I just looked at him. I couldn't believe what had happened. Eventually he gave us a puck, which we had to return after the warm-ups."

Van Impe told about another episode with Shore.

"Once while we were playing at Springfield, one of our players went crashing into the goalpost and tore a whole sheet of ice up. There was nothing left around the net but the cement floor. Shore wanted to continue playing, but the referee stopped the game with the score tied, 2–2, in the third period. The referee immediately called the league president and said that the game should not be continued under such conditions. So we went back to our locker room and began getting dressed when we learned that Shore himself had called the league president and talked him into making us finish the game. But our club had to take the bad end of the rink.

"We suited up and returned to the ice—it was about 11:30 at night. We hadn't been playing for more than a minute when we scored and won the game.

"As soon as the final buzzer sounded, Shore ran down from his box and grabbed the microphone for the arena loudspeaker and called the referee 'a plum'! I couldn't believe it."

Van Impe's patience was eventually rewarded when, in 1966, he received an invitation to the Black Hawks' training camp, along with a promise from coach Billy Reay that Ed would have a chance to make the club. "A man can't ask for anything more than a chance to make good," commented Van Impe, "and I got that chance." The 25-year-old rookie was teamed up on the blueline with Pat Stapleton, and he soon found his niche with Chicago. His first NHL game resulted in his first goal, the game-winning tally in a contest with the Canadiens. To top off his year, Ed finished second to Bobby Orr of the Bruins in the voting for the league's rookie-of-the-year. His reward? A send-off to Philadelphia in the expansion draft before the 1967–68 season. Almost incredibly, he expressed no resentment toward his former employers. "I have no bad feelings toward Chicago. I'm satisfied with Philadelphia."

The Flyers were more than satisfied with Van Impe. After leading Philadelphia to the West Division title in their maiden season, he was named captain of the Flyers for the 1968–69 campaign. "It's a big thrill to play in the NHL, but being named captain of an NHL team is quite an honor," he said. "I'm not a holler guy. The best way I can lead this team is to go out on the ice and help win some games." Ed's willingness to take the team's younger players aside and patiently instruct them contributed to his selection to the captaincy.

Van Impe has developed a quasi-sinister reputation for his indiscreet stickwork and meatgrinder philosophy. "I don't want other teams to push us around," he says. "The opposing forwards must respect us. I have to keep them wondering just what I might do." Nor is he loath to hurl his body in front of flying pucks. Ed's face was the victim of an Alex Delvecchio shot in 1967, and a blueline drive from Wayne Muloin of the Seals in 1970. The first injury required sixteen stitches, the second cost him six teeth and 35 stitches. Vic Stasiuk, coach of the Flyers at the time of Ed's first mishap, remarked, "Van Impe has a killer instinct. Not many hockey players would have done that. A guy who will make a move like that really comes to play the game."

Though Van Impe came to play the game, he found the captaincy was not his cup of tea. He voluntarily abdicated the position early in the 1971–72 season.

"Fred (coach Fred Shero) and I discussed it," Van Impe

explained. "We decided it would be in the best interest of the club if I just took care of myself and concentrated on doing my own job. If anyone needs advice, I'll be available." Ed praised the new captain, Bobby Clarke, and promptly began playing what his coach called, "the best defense in the league." Shero went on to say that Van Impe is "right up there with the most valuable players on this team."

Typically, Ed has not forgotten those who helped him make it to the top. "I owe a lot of thanks to Billy Reay, who coached me with the Black Hawks. He was soft-spoken, but when he spoke he had a point to make, and I discovered that he made a lot of sense."

He also has no regrets about the long years in the minors. "All that minor league experience helped me, and it will help me stay in the NHL a few more years. If I had come up to the majors earlier, I might well have been sent back down," he says. "In retrospect, I feel that those six years on the farm were worth every minute of it."

Six years in the minors, experience with a first-place team, and the jolt of beginning anew with an expansion club in its first season. All these ingredients have made Ed Van Impe the unobtrusive ace of the Flyers' blueline corps.

21/

Bernie Parent, Super Goalie

For the city of Philadelphia, it looked like the biggest thing since cream cheese. A bold-faced, eight-column banner headline in *The Philadelphia Inquirer* loudly proclaimed, PARENT COMES HOME!!! FLYERS SAY IT'S FOR GOOD!!

For Bernie Parent, still searching an answer to the burning question, "Why can't one of the best goalies in hockey find happiness in the City of Brotherly Love?," it was the third go-round in his bizarre love–hate relationship with the fair city of Philadelphia.

"I never wanted to leave here in the first place," confessed the 28-year-old goalie as he inked a new, multi-year contract with the Flyers on June 22, 1973. "Now that I'm back," he beamed, "I couldn't be happier."

Drafted from the Boston Bruins organization in 1967, Parent was the first player to join the Flyers in their first year of expansion. After having spent the previous two seasons shuffling between the Bruins and their Oklahoma City farm team, Parent was left unprotected in the draft in favor of the comical Gerry Cheevers.

At the Flyers training camp, Bernie found his competition to be an equally glib Doug Favell, whose acrobatic net tending style made Parent's classic stand-up approach to the game seem drab and colorless. To make matters worse, Favell's goals-against average was slightly lower than Bernie's and a dejected Parent spent more than half the season on the bench.

Despite his obvious disappointment, Parent turned in an impressive 2.49 goals-against average and four shutouts. The two young goalies led the Philly sextet to a first-place finish in the NHL's West Division, but it was Parent who was turning heads around the league.

"When the Flyers made the playoffs," observed the then-coach of the Oakland Seals, Fred Glover, "it was mostly thanks to Parent."

"Bernie is the best young goalie in the NHL," chimed in St. Louis coach Scotty Bowman as the Blues and Flyers prepared to do battle in the semi-finals of the Stanley Cup playoffs. "And when Glenn Hall and Jacques Plante retire, he'll be the best in the game."

Despite all the praise being heaped on Parent, it was Doug Favell who got the starting assignment for the opening game of the 1967–68 playoffs. Favell had finished the season with a slightly better average than his partner, but an eleventh hour illness suddenly thrust Parent into the forefront.

Usually an introspective worrier, Parent's attitude toward tending goal had changed drastically over the last year thanks to teammate Larry Zeidel.

During the regular season, Parent had been scheduled to guard the cage against the classy Canadiens at the Montreal

Forum. Flustered, Bernie spent a sleepless night nervously questioning his roomie, Zeidel.

"We don't have a chance do we? How many shots do you think they'll take at me?"

Zeidel, the cagey old veteran defenseman, was reading *Psycho-Cybernetics: A New Way To Get More Living Out of Life.*

"You've gotta think positive," he told Bernie. "Just let the old subconscious work for you."

Four hours later the Flyers were on the way home with a 4–1 win under their belts and a goalie with a new outlook on life.

"I'm not scared of being in the playoffs for the first time," insisted Parent as he prepared for the Blues. "One thing I don't fear is the pressure, because we faced all kinds of pressure the last six weeks of the season and still we finished first. We can win it."

Bernie's positive thinking paid off . . . almost. Only one puck managed to find its way over the Philadelphia goal line. But the Flyers lost the game 1–0. Philadelphia's anemic scoring punch was their undoing as Parent valiantly posted a miserly 1.35 goals-against average in a losing cause. The Flyers lost the series.

A season later Parent and Favell were friendly enemies once again as they vied for the No. 1 spot. One day in training camp, as a forward artfully slipped the puck between Bernie's pads and into the net, the goalie slammed his oversized stick against the goalpost in disgust, snapping it in two with a sharp *crackkk*.

"Barnyard!" bellowed Favell, doubled over with laughter, "you're nothing but a damn sorehead."

Actually, it's just the opposite. Bernie Parent is an easy-going, friendly sort of chap who has been known to raise his voice in song when his spirits are high, but not too high. Parent's fear of flying is surpassed only by Minnesota North Stars goalie Gump Worsley.

"Keith, Keith!" would be the panic-stricken scream from Parent's seat during a particularly bumpy flight. Keith Allen, then the Flyers' coach would make his way to Bernie's side to investigate.

"Keith, next time please let's take the train."

Despite Parent's fear of heights, he was showing that he had no problem at all stopping flying rubber. Favell was losing favor with the Flyer management, and when he was beaten six times in one game by Red Berenson during an 8–0 pasting from St. Louis, it was Bernie's cue to step forward. The Flyers were floundering precariously close to the West Division cellar, but with Parent between the pipes they staged a dramatic stretch drive for third place and a playoff berth.

The 1968–69 Stanley Cup quarter-final between St. Louis and Philadelphia was most brutal for the Flyers. They were set upon by the St. Louis Blues in the manner of a pack of wolves devouring a wounded fawn.

"It was a disgrace," recalls Larry Zeidel. "The Blues broke Claude Laforge's jaw, they broke Gary Dornhoefer's leg, and they just ran the Flyers out of the rink."

Philadelphia was beaten all the way back to the Spectrum in four straight games. Flyer general manager Bud Poile, in desperate need of firepower, was issued an ultimatum by the club brass: "Make a deal or else!"

Parent, now firmly established as the Flyers' chief netminder, posted a respectable 2.79 goals-against average in 62 games during 1969–70. The only problem was that Philadelphia scorers averaged 2.58 goals per game and the Flyers finished in fifth place—out of the playoffs.

Midway through the 1970–71 season, forced to deal for offensive power, the Flyers traded Parent to the Toronto Maple Leafs for center Mike Walton and goalie Bruce Gamble. Walton was then dealt to Boston for Rick MacLeish. Parent was shocked and disappointed. He had established firm roots in Philadelphia and had grown to be a favorite with the fans.

But, looking on the positive side, the Maple Leafs were in fourth place in the tough East Division with a shot at the Stanley Cup and Bernie would finally be playing with his boyhood idol—Jacques Plante.

Plante and Parent complemented each other classically as the finest youth-experience goaltending combination in the league. They were to be the hopes of the Leafs against the precise passing of the New York Rangers in the Stanley Cup quarter-final.

It was Plante, the wise old master, guarding the goal for Toronto in the first game, with a wild scoring spree that had the Rangers hanging on for a 5–4 win. Bernie donned the pads for the second game and was holding the New Yorkers at bay 4–1 late in the third period when a flare-up erupted along the right boards.

There was still bad blood in the air over the first game's roughhouse tactics and immediately all twelve skaters closed in on the shoving match. Parent, bolting from the crease, vigorously checked Ranger bad boy Vic Hadfield into the boards, bringing a chorus of lusty Bronx cheers from the vast towers of Madison Square Garden. Hadfield, struggling for something to grab onto, ripped Parent's custom-made mask off the shocked goalie's cherubic face and sailed it high into the first promenade.

Frantically, Bernie strained at the sideboards, imploring the sea of faces before him to return the mask. His answer came quickly in the form of a droning, rhythmic chant, "Don't give it back, Don't give it back!"

When it was obvious that the Garden majority ruled, Parent shrugged his shoulders and yielded to Plante, who finished out the remaining few minutes. Parent's spare mask was still hanging in the trainer's room at Maple Leaf Gardens in Toronto and Bernie had no desire to risk his pearly whites.

New York's superior firepower began to tell after Bernie beat the Rangers again in Toronto for a 2–1 lead in the series. From then on New York did not lose as Toronto's youthful defensive corps betrayed the Maple Leaf netminders time after time. When it was all over and the Leafs had been defeated four games to two, Parent received a parcel from New York City. It was the celebrated mask, returned only when Bernie could be of no more harm to the Broadway Blueshirts.

The Leafs goaltending combination of Plante and Parent split time in 1971–72 with Bernie getting the nod for 47 games and posting a 2.56 goals per game yield. But trouble was brewing. Bernie's wife, Carol, a native Philadelphian, did not like the cold weather in Toronto. There was another matter too, an intruder called the World Hockey Association.

In desperate need of credibility, the new league was looking for proven players and said they had the money to do some hard talking. Bernie listened, and before you could say "slapshot," an outfit with the flamboyant handle of "THE MIAMI SCREAMING EAGLES" announced the signing of the league's first superstar—Bernard Marcel Parent.

Miami sportspages, more familiar with greyhounds than goalposts, did not exactly welcome Bernie with open arms. Instead, they asked: "WHAT IS HOCKEY, AND WHO IS BERNIE PARENT?" Well, that showed everyone what Miami knew about the game and before you could say Fontainbleu the MIAMI SCREAMING EAGLES were the PHILADELPHIA PHANTOMS, and then finally, the PHILADELPHIA BLAZERS.

So, before the first WHA puck was ever dropped, Bernie Parent had signed two WHA contracts! Bernie became the Blazer's hope for a successful franchise. He had negotiated a fat contract through his lawyer, Howard Casper, and best of all, he was back in Philadelphia.

With the ancient Marcel Paille as the Blazers No. 2 goaltender, most of the workload was on Bernie's shoulders. After an early season injury, he finished the inaugural WHA campaign by appearing in 57 consecutive games and chalking up the most victories in the entire league with 33.

During the season some ugly namecalling arose between Parent and his crosstown ex-employers, the Flyers. Parent was peeved at the Flyers who, in the midst of booming attendance figures, were looking down their noses at the Blazers.

"The Flyers right now are nothing better than a fourth or fifth place team," spouted an incensed Parent. "I honestly don't think they're any better now than they were before."

Parent did not express any personal animosity toward the players, in fact, he still maintained friendships with his exteammates.

"I gave a few guys a lift to the Spectrum last summer and they asked me inside," Bernie recalled. "When I went in and saw the look on some of the faces (of the Flyers brass), I said I'd rather wait in the car."

It is the Flyers, Bernie claims, who hardened his heart when he was traded to Toronto.

"They trade you like that—snap! They show you they don't want you," he said bitterly.

But then right in the middle of the WHA playoff quarter-finals against the Cleveland Crusaders, with the Blazers down one game to none, Bernie decided to demonstrate his discontent. A bombshell exploded on the nation's sports pages.

According to Parent's lawyer, a $600,000 check serving as the guarantee on Parent's lucrative contract was withdrawn from the bank without Bernie's knowledge. This, said Parent's attorney, voided his client's contract and Bernie would not play under these circumstances. A Mexican standoff followed with the Philadelphia hockey fans clearly the losers. With rookie goaler Yves Archambault thrown into the breach, the Blazers were obliterated in four straight games.

The Blazers' playoff fiasco was quickly followed by a statement from the club vowing that Parent would never play for the team again. This, in turn, was quickly followed by the Blazers departure from Philadelphia for the great northwest of Vancouver. Parent and high-scoring center Andre Lacroix were shipped to the New York Golden Blades in exchange for Ron Ward and Pete Donnelly.

Having resettled in Philly, the prospect of another move did not sit well with the Parents. After extensive negotiations with both the Golden Blades and the local NHL Flyers,

Bernie was welcomed back to the Spectrum with open arms and visions of Stanley Cups in the Summer of 1973.

Recalling his barbs aimed at the Flyer management, Bernie turned apologetic. "I made mistakes," he admitted. "I've learned a lot since then. The Flyers treated me pretty good.

"The Golden Blades made me a pretty good deal. As a matter of fact, I took a cut coming to the Flyers."

Thomas Wolfe once wrote a book entitled *You Can't Go Home Again*. But he wasn't writing about Philadelphia; nor was he Bernie Parent.

Puffing on a big black cigar, Parent concludes: "I've always considered myself a Flyer."

22/

Dave Schultz, the Hammer

Once upon a time the Philadelphia Flyers were pussycats.
In the 1969 Stanley Cup series against the St. Louis Blues,
for example, the Flyers were eliminated in four straight
games. That happened primarily because of intimidation.
Tough defensemen like the Plager brothers and Noel Picard
would throw a couple of mean looks, and the smaller, lighter,
and less-violent Flyers would back off.

That, as far as general manager Keith Allen was concerned, carried Brotherly Love just a bit too far. So, he
decided to add some muscle. He has succeeded to the point
where the Flyers are now known as the Mad Squad . . . the
Broad Street Bullies . . . and Freddie's Philistines—the last
in honor of coach Fred Shero.

The Mad Squad is made up of Bob Kelly, Don Saleski,
André Dupont, and Dave Schultz, also known as The En-
forcer. He is the baddest of Philadelphia's Bad Guys. And he
likes it.

"I doubt if I'd ever made it in the NHL if I'd done otherwise," Schultz admits candidly. "I have a role to play. If

somebody goes after a player like (Bobby) Clarke, my job is to punish the guy."

Last season was Schultz' first in the NHL and it was marked by some memorable fights. Against Serge Savard of the Montreal Canadiens, he split, losing the first but winning the second by a wide margin when Savard was forced to the dressing room for eight stitches in his face.

Schultz also scored a lop-sided decision over Steve Durbano of the St. Louis Blues. Durbano had accumulated more penalty minutes in a single season in the minor leagues than had Schultz. Dave took this as a personal insult, and so promptly settled the score.

But perhaps his best fights of his rookie year were against Montreal's Pierre Bouchard. Bouchard won the first but Schultz came out on top in the second.

"It was a good fight," Schultz said of the rematch. "It's always a good fight when two guys can stand up there and throw."

Said Bouchard: "I don't think I was beaten, but I didn't look good."

What is somewhat surprising about Schultz' emergence as one of the NHL's leading tough guys is the almost total absence of violence in his background. Dave grew up in a middle-class neighborhood in Rosetown, Saskatchewan, one of five children of a garage mechanic. And he was a relatively peaceful young man until he went to play junior hockey in Sorel, Quebec.

"I never had a fight off the ice," he explains, "no gang stuff or anything like that.

"I used to go to a guy's house back home with my brother Ray (who plays with Syracuse in the Eastern League),"

Schultz recalls. "The guy had boxing gloves and I used to get the hell beat out of me."

But with Sorel he learned that a rough team can be very successful. He really didn't hit his stride, though, until he joined the Salem Beavers of the Eastern League.

"I got into a fight and won and I just kept going from there," Schultz says. "It was really effective, too. We went from last place to second in one year."

For that 1969–70 campaign Schultz had 32 goals and 37 assists. He also had 356 minutes in penalties, which was a new league record.

The following year with the Quebec Aces of the American Hockey League he had 14 goals and 23 assists. And he also scored 382 minutes in penalties for a new AHL mark.

The season after that at Richmond he had 18 goals and 28 assists and 392 minutes in penalties. This broke the league record he had set the year before, and prompted his promotion to the Flyers.

"I wasn't sure at the beginning that Schultz would even make the team," coach Shero says now. "But as the season progressed I realized that his being physical helped us."

Or, as Allen puts it: "Dave stimulates our hockey club."

Schultz also stimulates the crowds. At the Spectrum, of course, he can do no wrong. Out-of-town, it's a different matter. During a game last season against the North Stars, for example, Schultz was drenched by a water pistol, bopped on the head with a program, and threatened by fans sitting behind the penalty box, where Dave spent a good part of the evening.

"Then (Dennis) Hextall speared me in the throat after the whistle," Dave recalls. "Another inch over and I could have been hurt seriously. Sure I fight, but I'd never try purposely to hurt a guy. We're all in this together. Maybe Hextall knew what he was doing but it was too close for me."

Later, in a playoff game at Minnesota, the fans jeered every time Schultz skated near the boards during the warm-ups. Angered, Schultz slammed his stick against the protective glass. At which point thousands of fans started chanting: "We hate Schultz . . . We hate Schultz!"

In some other NHL cities, such as Montreal, the hatred has gone even further. Prior to one of the playoff games against the Canadiens, a Montreal radio station received a call. The caller, who spoke French, warned: "Schultz will never get out of the Forum alive."

Before and after the game, Schultz was under heavy police guard. But the anonymous caller never made good on his threat, and Schultz played his normal uninhibited game.

For Schultz, being one of the NHL's Bad Guys is a two-edged sword. He admits he enjoys the attention and notoriety.

"I was just as bad or worse in the American League but there was never any national publicity like this," he says. "Still, I like the challenge. I like trying to outsmart the other teams and their fans when they get on me."

But the ill-will he generates in enemy camps can at times be disturbing.

"What really bothers me is the little kids swearing at me," Schultz says. "Why pick on me? I'm only human. I've got feelings."

Coach Shero doesn't worry about the little kids picking on Schultz. What bothers him is the feeling that the referees are starting to pick on Dave.

"The refs are so scared they can't even referee anymore," Shero claimed. "They can't watch the play because they're looking for Schultz. Are there special rules for Schultz? Now the refs are trying to coach the teams."

Schultz did spend 259 minutes in the penalty box his rookie year in the NHL. But as Montreal coach Scotty Bowman pointed out, the type of penalty Schultz takes normally does not hurt his team.

"Schultz doesn't put his team in trouble because he usually takes a man off the ice with him," Bowman says. "He had 19 major penalties, 10 misconducts and 10 to 15 minors involving a player from the other team. That means the Flyers were shorthanded for only about 30 of his 259 minutes in the box this season."

Schultz has one weakness. He does not skate well. Shero, in fact, has suggested that Schultz might benefit from figure skating lessons in the off season. General manager Allen, while recognizing Schultz' limitations, still believes he will be around the NHL for many years.

"I hate to keep referring to John Ferguson, the ex-Montreal badman, but that's who Schultz reminds me of," Allen says. "Fergie wasn't a great skater, but what an asset he was to his team."

Ferguson's team was a champion. Until his retirement a few years ago, Ferguson was the most feared of hockey's Bad Guys.

"There's no reason why Dave can't be as good as Ferguson," Allen says. "When he makes a good move you can bet that nobody's going to drape themselves all over him because they don't want to take a chance on what follows."

During his career, Ferguson became something of a loner.

It's like being the top gun in the Old West. There's always someone new coming along looking to make his reputation at your expense.

"The big thing you're scared of is really getting beaten in a fight," Schultz admits. "A lot of guys never get over it. That's what happened to Earl Heiskala when he was here a couple of years ago. Keith Magnuson of the Hawks really unloaded on him. Gave him a 20-stitch job on the face and Heiskala never got over it.

"Me, I've been in fights where there was no way I won," Schultz says. "But there's no way I got the hell kicked out of me, either. I don't know how I'd react if I really got the hell kicked out of me. I hope I never have to find out."

23/

Bill Barber,
New Kid on Campus

Bill Barber did not win the Calder Cup in 1972–73. But he did win the hearts of Flyer fans.

The Cup, of course, is awarded to the NHL's Rookie of the Year. Steve Vickers of the New York Rangers got it. But coach Fred Shero believes it could just as easily have gone to Barber, who topped all of the first-year players in scoring with 30 goals and 34 assists.

"Vickers is a type, a good goal scorer," Shero explained. "He's got a good touch around the net, something like (ex-Ranger) Camille Henry, who was positively great around the net. Vickers may turn out to be a great hockey player because of his size and touch around the net.

"But," Shero continues, "I still think Barber is and will continue to be a better all-around hockey player. It takes all kinds to make a hockey team, hitters and scorers.

"We needed a guy who could do everything," Shero adds. "New York could have done very well without Vickers. We couldn't do without Barber."

General manager Keith Allen seconds the Shero motion.

"I just think Bill turned out to be a helluva hockey player," Allen says. "Like Jimmy Roberts (of the Canadiens) remarked at the end of the 1973 Cup series with Montreal, he just didn't realize what a great hockey player this kid was, how strong he was, and what a good skater he was. I thought it was a great tribute to Barber."

Bill was Philadelphia's first choice in the 1972 NHL amateur draft. A native of Callander, Ontario, and one of five brothers, Bill was encouraged to play hockey by his father, who hoped that at least one of his sons would make it to the NHL.

"Just to make sure we had everything going for us, Dad built us a rink that was almost regulation size, had hydro poles put up, and lights strung out."

There was one catch. Bill and his brothers were responsible for clearing the ice.

"It snows a lot up there, and you'd just get through ploughing a foot of it off the rink, and it'd start again—and you had to clear off another foot of it," Barber recalls. "I think all that ploughing was the thing that made my arms as strong as they are."

Barber was selected by the Flyers after he had spent three years with the Kitchener juniors in the OHA. During that time he had 127 goals and 171 assists, while playing both the center and forward spots.

He expected to make the Flyers without any trouble, but was farmed out to Richmond before the start of last season because his checking was not up to NHL standards.

"I never thought checking in the NHL was so hard or important," Barber said. "There's a world of difference between Richmond and here. You wouldn't believe all the breakaways I had in Richmond."

Barber spent a month there, then was brought up by the Flyers to replace Bill Flett, who was out of action because of a sprained knee. Barber failed to score in his first few games, but played well enough to continue taking regular turns.

"Then we played Buffalo and won, 5–3, and I got two goals and two assists," Barber recalls. "That clinched it for me."

For a couple of months Bill played left wing on a line with Rick MacLeish and Gary Dornhoefer. Then he was teamed with Bill Flett and Bobby Clarke.

"Bobby really helped me a lot," Barber said. "He wants me to carry the puck out. He knows the game as well as anybody. And if I'm in the open, I can be sure Bobby will have it on my stick.

"When I had 29 goals, Bobby Clarke sacrificed everything for me," Barber continued. "Every time I looked up I saw the puck. He just kept feeding me and feeding me. What a guy."

Even though Barber has had limited NHL service, Shero thinks so highly of him that he is willing to compare Bill with one of the league's all-time greats, former Ranger Andy Bathgate.

"As soon as Bill stepped out on the ice you knew he was a hockey player and was going to be better than most of the others. He had the same sort of class and finesse with the puck, and the hockey brains, that Bathgate had.

"And when some of the other teams started to challenge Bill he fought back, and fought back well. Bathgate, you'll remember, was quite a fighter himself, one of the best."

Shero expects that Barber will continue to improve . . . which is quite an order.

"First of all, I expect him to play a rougher type game," Shero explains.

"He knows that I want him to contribute more, that I want him to kill penalties, as well as taking his regular shift and working on power plays," Shero adds.

"He also knows he may to have to center a third line if we can't come up with anyone. Bill knows he'll be counted on more than he was last season."

If Barber does not live up to Shero's expectations, it will not be for lack of trying. He is the type of competitor, for example, who played part of his rookie season with a broken toe. That takes discipline.

"Why do I discipline myself?" Barber says. "It's pretty simple really. I still have a scared feeling. I keep thinking, 'What if I don't produce?' "

And he knows that his educational process has only begun.

"You learn things in this league you just wouldn't believe could happen," Barber explains. "Several times in my rookie season Dorny (Dornhoefer) and Rick (MacLeish) put the puck on my stick when I didn't believe they could get it to me. And because I was so surprised I didn't react fast enough to take advantage of it. That's learning the hard way."

Some people feel that Barber's chances for Rookie of the Year honors would have been improved if he'd gotten more publicity. A few even suggested that a gimmick might have helped—something like Flett's beard, for example. But that's not Barber's style.

"I was talking to my dad and he said it would have been nice if I'd won the Calder Cup," Barber recalls. "Sure it would have been nice . . . who wouldn't want it. But every game I was just trying to concentrate.

"Actually," he concluded, "I never thought about it before my first season. My only goals were to make the NHL and play with Philadelphia."

24/

Bill Flett,
the Bearded Wonder

Bill Flett's NHL career has been marked by peaks and valleys. Following the 1972–73 season, he was "King of the Hill"—coming off a 43-goal year for the Flyers.

But just a few short years before—while he was still with the Los Angeles Kings—"Cowboy" Bill suffered through a 13-goal season. That probably had a lot to do with the trade sending him, Ross Lonsberry, Jean Potvin, and Eddie Joyal to the Flyers in exchange for Serge Bernier, Bill Lesuk, Jimmy Johnson, and Larry Brown.

The trade took place on January 28, 1972. It was almost a year before the Flyers and their fans realized just how important it was. In between, a few things happened.

First, Flett jumped to the New York Raiders of the World Hockey Association. "It was strictly a matter of money," Flett admits. "The WHA offered me more, so I went. But the Flyers kept talking to me in an effort to get me to return. And I returned because I got the kind of money that made me happy.

"Sure, it's a sport, but it's also a job," Flett continued, quite candidly. "Most working men will go to work where they get the most money."

Once back with Philadelphia, Flett decided to grow the longest hair, beard, and sideburns yet seen in the NHL. Of the three, the beard remained his pride and joy.

"I grew it in the hospital when I had to have some surgery," Flett says. "My wife liked it, so I kept it."

Some NHL coaches might well frown on a bearded player. Not Fred Shero, who is quite realistic about the whole hirsuite thing.

"As long as he keeps playing well, I don't care what he does with his hair," Shero explained. "There are more important things than hair. Besides, there are other guys on this team who will have to get haircuts before Flett has to shave."

Flett's new image, however, did not go over as well in Los Angeles. The problem was that Kings' fans look upon Flett as something of a traitor, even though it was the club's management, and not Flett, which instituted the trade that sent the Cowboy east. So, when Flett made his first appearance at the Forum in Los Angeles in 1972–73, he was roundly booed.

"They hate me and they have ever since I came to Philadelphia," Flett says. "The fans were on my back right from the beginning.

"I didn't mind it so much," he continued, reliving the incident, "but I didn't like them giving it to my wife, too. Some of the fans really let her have it."

To get even, Flett stood at center ice, looked up at the stands, and scratched his beard; slowly, caressingly, Flett scratched his beard and drove the LA fans wild. They booed; oh, how they booed. But Flett managed to silence them by the end of the game. He did so by scoring two goals, the second at 19:29 of the third period. That one gave the Flyers a 4–3 win.

Flett, in fact, had a great many pressure goals. Eleven of his 43 goals came on power plays. Another three were scored while the Flyers were short-handed. And six of the goals won games for Philadelphia.

With 31 assists to go with his 43 goals, Flett was the highest-scoring wing in the West Division. Never before in his professional career had he even approached such figures.

Flett broke in with the Charlotte Checkers of the Eastern Hockey League in 1963–64 and had 26 goals and 21 assists in 41 games. His season was cut short by a severe leg cut.

After bouncing around the Western and American hockey leagues for two seasons, Flett found a permanent home with the Tulsa Oilers of the Central League. He missed part of the 1965–66 campaign with a broken wrist and a portion of the 1966–67 season with mononucleosis. His goal output for the two years was 39.

Flett made it to the NHL in the first year of expansion, when the Kings drafted him from the Toronto Maple Leafs' organization. With Los Angeles, Flett had 26 goals and 20 assists and he was named Rookie of the Year in the Western Division by *The Sporting News*.

The following season (1968–69) Flett scored 24 goals and added 25 assists. But just when it appeared that he might be on the verge of NHL stardom, it all came apart.

Flett managed just 14 goals in 1969–70 and 13 in 1970–71. He was traded to Philadelphia after 45 games of the 1971–72 season, at which point he had but seven goals for the Kings.

Actually, the Flyers expected more from Joyal than Flett; but it was Flett who made the greater contribution. And one reason for this, perhaps, was because of the way the Flyers' management treated him.

After his jump back to the Flyers, for example, general manager Keith Allen said: "We're very happy to have Bill back. Whatever he may have signed with the Raiders was strictly a business deal. He never knocked us. He admitted we made him a good offer. He never closed the door on us."

But he soon was closing the door on Philadelphia's opponents. Flett had 25 goals by the All-Star break, even though he missed three weeks because of a knee injury. As he neared the 40-goal plateau, Flett played it cool.

"Start thinking about stuff like that and it can only throw you off," Flett remarked at the time. "You just come out every night and play your game."

Those are the words of a professional, and Flett is every bit that. At 6'1", 195 pounds Flett is an aggressive checker with "a shot like a bullet," according to Shero. Yet for all his ruggedness Flett does not draw that many penalties. He served only 53 minutes last season, and he and Bobby Clarke, as a team, were Philadelphia's top penalty-killers. Due to the Flyers' physical style of play, Flett and Clarke spent a good deal of time on the ice in short-handed situations.

"We're going to have to cut down on those penalties," Flett commented after the season was over. "We're going to get crucified by the teams that can work the power play."

Not that Flett was advocating a change in style for the Flyers. Nor was he being critical of some of his more penalty-prone teammates. He does believe, however, that a number of the league's referees are a bit too sensitive when it comes to the way the Flyers now play the game.

"Maybe we're talking to some of the referees too much, doing too much griping," Flett observes. "It's tough to do, at least for me, but maybe we're going to have to cut down on our conversation."

It appears, however, that Cowboy will not "cut down" any on his beard . . . or his sideburns . . . or his long hair.

"I'm in great shape and I feel strong," Flett explains. "A guy is supposed to get strength from his hair and if I cut mine I might lose my strength."

The Cowboy also points out that having the great Bobby Clarke for a center is a big help as well.

"Bobby deserves a lot of the credit for the way I've been playing," Flett says seriously. Then, tongue in cheek, he adds:

"Still, there may be something to this hair bit after all."

25/

Gary Dornhoefer, All Tough

Back in 1967, when the Philadelphia Flyers were born via the expansion draft, twenty players were selected. Some were terribly young and inexperienced. Others were aging and obviously over-the-hill. A few were of major league caliber.

All had one thing in common, however. They were found by the six established NHL clubs to be expendable. They were, in effect, castoffs. So, it is not surprising that most of the players picked in that original expansion draft are no longer around the NHL.

One who has survived is Gary Dornhoefer. He is, in fact, the only one of the original Flyer forwards still with the team. And there's a reason for that. In his six seasons with the Flyers, Gary has developed into one of the West Division's steadiest two-way players. With 290 points, he became Philadelphia's all-time scoring leader. In 1972–73 he scored 30 goals and added 49 assists—which were single-season highs for him in both departments.

Yet, Dornhoefer's value to the team goes beyond statistics. He is, with Bobby Clarke, really the "heart" of the Philadelphia club. A veteran player who has matured along with the Flyers, he is truly a well-rounded professional who puts the team above individual accomplishment.

"I'm sure winning helps, but I think it's believing in the guys you're with," Dornhoefer says, explaining Philadelphia's recent success. "We have 20 guys who believe we can win. Everybody believes in everybody else. I just believe in everybody out there."

So there is togetherness on the Flyers. And coach Fred Shero believes that Dornhoefer deserves a lion's share of the credit for that.

"He became a leader," says Shero. "He encouraged the other guys. They look up to him and they like him. When we need a lift he'll go in and work twice as hard."

Dornhoefer and Shero have been through some lean times together. Not too long ago Shero confessed that he felt more like a camp counselor than a major league hockey coach. Fred, for example, likes to tell about some of the excuses he would hear when one of his players had not performed up to Shero's expectations . . . which were never all that high anyway.

"One guy tells me the reason he's not skating well is because he hasn't got a pair of skates," Shero recalls. "I couldn't believe my ears. The guy could go out and buy any pair he wants made-to-measure and have the bill sent to the Flyers.

"Instead," Shero continues, "he borrows a left skate from one player and a right skate from another. I only found out by accident. I swear, there were times you could have cried."

Dornhoefer's memories are somewhat similar.

"I've been through it all with this club," he says. "We've lost in the playoffs in four straight, we've lost in seven games and we've missed the playoffs in the last four seconds of the season.

"I want to be here when we win the Stanley Cup," he adds, "and we're going in the right direction."

Gary was drafted by the Flyers from the Boston Bruins, for whom he had played part-time for three seasons with a minimum of success.

Dornhoefer had first joined the Bruins in 1963–64 after two years of junior hockey and a half-season in the minor leagues. And he bounced between Boston and the minors until rescued from hockey oblivion by expansion and the Flyers.

Reviewing Dornhoefer's performance during his first two years with the Flyers, it seemed that Boston's decision to dump him had been an excellent one. In 1967–68 Gary had 13 goals. The following season he had just eight. Not surprisingly, the Flyers left him unprotected in the draft of 1969, but no other team claimed him.

At that point Dornhoefer probably realized that his future in the NHL was on thin ice. And he responded to the challenge with 26 goals and 29 assists during the 1969–70 campaign.

"Gary has come a long way," says former Flyers' defenseman, Larry Zeidel. "He has polished up his game. He has a more accurate shot.

"One of his problems used to be that he'd get frustrated and take bad shots," Zeidel added. "But now he's a smarter hockey player and a good competitor."

Zeidel also points out that Dornhoefer was a fine defensive

forward almost from the moment he entered the NHL.

"For me it was easy playing defense with the Flyers because I had a guy like Dornhoefer back-checking on the wing," Zeidel said. "When he had to cover Bobby Hull, for example, he'd be on him early and he'd be on him all the way.

"You weren't outnumbered; it wasn't the centerman and the winger against you," Zeidel continued. "Gary was always coming back, and he was a tremendous forechecker, too. He could keep his job on his defensive ability alone."

Leg injuries forced Dornhoefer to miss 19 games during the 1970–71 season and, consequently, his scoring output was down from the previous season—just 20 goals and 20 assists. The following year he managed only 17 goals, but did have 32 assists. And 1972–73, of course, was his best by far.

"We still feel that Gary doesn't shoot enough," Shero says. "But on a line with (Rick) MacLeish, I don't see why he can't get another 30 goals for us any season."

That's a large order. But it's not at all impossible. Certainly, Dornhoefer has done everything expected of him over the past few seasons. When the Flyers got tougher as a team, for example, so did Dornhoefer. His aggressiveness accounted for 183 minutes in the penalty box in 1971–72, and 168 minutes the next season. Shero also uses Gary on power plays and killing penalties.

In the course of 1972–73 Dornhoefer also was named to the West team for the annual All-Star game and he came close to equaling the NHL mark for scoring goals in consecutive games.

The record—held jointly by Andy Bathgate, who did it

for the Rangers, and Bobby Hull, who did it for the Black Hawks—is 10. Dornhoefer came within three games of joining that select company. His string, in fact, was broken on a controversial scoring play against the Bruins at the Spectrum.

What happened was that defenseman Joe Watson let fly from just inside the blue line. The puck went into the net and some press box observers thought it did so on a deflection off Dornhoefer's pads.

"I couldn't say for sure because quite honestly I didn't feel a thing," Dornhoefer said after the game. "If we were able to look at films, maybe it would show I did touch it last. But no movies were taken, so I guess we'll never know for sure.

"Aw, heck," he decided, "I wouldn't want the goal that way, anyway. I want to work for it."

During the off-season Gary is a golf pro. Among NHL players he is probably the best of the golfers, and when his hockey career is over he plans to join the professional tour. A few years back, he actually considered giving up hockey for golf. Now he's glad he didn't. It would have meant missing the 1972–73 season. It would have also meant missing one of the greatest ovations accorded an athlete at the Spectrum.

It happened in a Stanley Cup playoff game against the Minnesota North Stars. Jack Chevalier of *The Philadelphia Bulletin* described it this way:

"In the pressure of Stanley Cup playoff sudden death, Dorny blasted through the Minnesota defense and backhanded a shot past Cesare Maniago to beat the North Stars, 3–2, after 8 minutes 35 seconds of overtime. The Spectrum crowd of 16,600 reacted with a leaping, arm-waving, 'from the heart' ovation. It was probably the most exciting individual play by a Philly athlete since Dick Sisler beat the Dodgers in Brooklyn with that home run in 1950 and gave the Phillies the pennant."

"Yeah, they were yelling a bit," said Dornhoefer recalling the moment. "It was the loudest cheer I've heard in Philadelphia."

The Flyers went on to defeat the North Stars in that opening round series and then gave the Canadiens fits before being ousted in five games. After the Canadien series Shero called Gary "the best, most competitive player on ice." And Dornhoefer, while saddened by the loss of the Montreal series, was far from discouraged.

"Everybody worked as hard as he could," Gary commented. "Montreal had a great club. They put the puck in the net when it counted and we couldn't get it past (Ken) Dryden.

"But we shouldn't be disappointed in the season," he continued. "If there's anything to be disappointed about, it's not being able to win at home after those great ovations.

"That was my most satisfying season ever. We had a good bunch of guys. A team."

26/

Marcel Pelletier, the Jester

The Philadelphia Flyers' press guide lists Marcel Pelletier as director of player personnel and says this about him: "During his pro career as a goaltender, Marcel won a total of six championships while playing with 13 different teams." What the press guide does not tell you is that the majority of those 13 teams were minor league . . . that he played in Vancouver and Los Angeles before they were NHL cities . . . that he was a journeyman goaltender.

Yet, for all of that, Pelletier is probably better remembered by those who played with him than most of the NHL's All-Star goalies are remembered by their teammates. He was a major leaguer in every respect.

Consider, for example, what happened when Marcel was hired as the spare goaltender for all playoff games in the Western League back in the early 1960s—a time when each team used just one goalie. Most players would have been content to remain in the background, collect their money for doing nothing, and then go home. Not Marcel Pelletier.

At each of the stops made by the teams he happened to be

travelling with, Marcel would unload a suitcase full of the finest liquors and set up bar in his room. There also were chairs and a card table. And each and every night he held open house for the players on both teams.

"I was getting paid for nozzing," he explained in his French-English twang at the time, "so is only fair to spread it among the boys, no?" And then in a burst of irrefutable logic, he continued: "I have dem all up because I never know which team I may be playing for . . . or against. Is true I no drink booze, but it is dere for those who want it. One has to be a good host, no? Besides, Marcel, he like companee."

Like many men with a flair for living, Marcel often refers to himself in the third person. But everything else about him is first. He dresses first class, dines first class, speaks first class and, of course, spends money first class.

"Most of zese guys," he has said, referring to his colleagues, "they got short arms and long pockets. They give you the spot off their shirt, they will."

Now, given Marcel's flamboyant style, it is somewhat surprising that he has ended up in a key position with one of the most successful of the NHL's expansion teams. Because hockey's establishment seldom takes well to a player who swings his way through life, cool and elegant, somewhat disdainful of those in authority.

Some years back, for instance, when he was tending goal for the minor-league Los Angeles Blades, Pelletier and two teammates were just finishing dinner at a posh restaurant as coach Lynn Patrick walked in.

"Jeez, you guys don't do bad on six bucks a day," Patrick remarked. To which Pelletier replied: "Where the brass goes, we go!"

Yet, for all of his brash manner and devil-may-care attitude, Pelletier also had within him a streak of shrewdness that serves him well in the job of judging and handling players of diverse talents, moods, wants, and needs.

Back in 1949, when Pelletier went to his first NHL training camp, with the Chicago Black Hawks, he asked if he could participate in the afternoon poker games presided over by the veteran players. "Awfully steep," one of the older Hawks told Marcel. But Marcel persisted and the veterans relented and at the end of the session he was up $250. Quite naturally he was invited back. This went on for five or six afternoons and each afternoon Marcel came out a winner.

Eventually the day came when Marcel arrived to pluck his pigeons only to be told that he was too late, the table was full. A few days of this and Marcel called a local cab company. After practice the following day Marcel dressed hurriedly, raced to the cab waiting for him outside the practice rink and went directly to the hotel. When the veterans arrived Marcel already was at the table.

"Marcel, he is early today," Pelletier said. And he was "early" for all of the other poker games during the remainder of training camp. He did not make the team, but he did come out a couple of thousand dollars ahead.

Given his expensive tastes and zest for life, one would presume that Marcel was raised in wealth. Not so. He was born December 6, 1927, in Drummondville, Quebec, and brought up in Sorel, Quebec. That's a town fairly close to Montreal in terms of distance, but light years away in terms of style, economics, and opportunity. Marcel's father was a boilermaker and Marcel made up his mind at an early age that he would not follow in his father's footsteps.

So, as a youngster, he tended goal on frozen streets or in outdoor rinks, even though the temperature often dropped to 20 degrees below zero. "It beat working," Marcel recalls.

He turned pro in 1949, played six games with the Black Hawks in 1950 and three with the Rangers in 1962. Otherwise it was the minor leagues, places like Chicoutimi, Victoria, Baltimore, and Seattle. He pays that no mind at all.

"If Marcel been der," he says, "dey remember, you bet dey do."

He also explains that he probably would have made it to the NHL had he been born 20 years later.

"Years ago, when Marcel at his best, the teams, zey carry only one goaler," he points out. "Marcel not ze best, though not ze worst, eithair. Now, every team, she carry two, three goaler. A young Marcel, he play, maybe star."

And, in fact, he did have his times of glory. Three times he topped various leagues in shutouts, and twice in fewest goals allowed. Several times he was an All-Star selection. He also was one of the first of the so-called "wandering goalies." But unlike some of his contemporaries, who would simply clear the puck to the sideboards or to a teammate standing close by, Pelletier went them one better by launching fast breaks with long lead passes that sometimes led to goals. More than once he had two assists in a single game.

He also was a master at stopping penalty shots. In his years in the Western League Marcel was beaten only once in 19 penalty shot attempts. On one occasion he skated out of the net and batted the puck away from his opponent before the player could shoot.

"He look for girl friend in the crowd, he no see me, so I make move," Marcel says recounting the incident. "Suddenly we both standing over the puck. Once I touch puck, shot over, but he mus' touch puck first, and he no have done that.

"What can I do? I no can turn my back on him and skate back. So, veree quicklee I bat puck away and skate to referee and say, the penalty shot is over, no, and the referee say, she is over, yes, and he wave teams back on the ice."

Marcel chuckles at the memory of it all.

"Referee, he wrong, but he no know it. Other player know it. He go crazee mad, but Marcel, he veree hapee."

Marcel never wore a mask and has 250 stitches in his face to show for it. He was somewhat rotund even while playing, packing 180 pounds on a 5'8" frame. But he liked the extra weight.

"It softened up ze puck when it hit you," he explains. "Besides, ze more of you to fill up the net, ze better, no?"

Finally, the years caught up with Marcel and he retired from competition. At first he thought he might become a referee.

"Being ref is a challenge," he says. "If you get everyone home happy, you do hell of a job. But I'm too old now for all the skating refs have to do."

He also considered coaching.

"Coaching is really a challenge, too," he says. "Have 17, 18 different men, each has to be treated different. Some coaches treat player all alike. Some player fool around when is not time to fool around. Player not give everyzing, he no play for Marcel."

But he ended up an executive with the Flyers.

In the front office, as on the ice, Marcel Pelletier is very much the professional. But more than that he is a unique personality, a man of humor and grace in a world of speed and violence. A man who knows his own worth.

Some years back, on a train ride between minor-league towns, Marcel showed up in the dining car looking at ease in clothes that were perfectly cut and neatly pressed. For breakfast he had steak and all the trimmings, even though he was receiving just $3 in meal money for the whole day.

Breakfast finished, he leaned back and lighted a 50-cent cigar.

"Ah," Marcel said. "Dere ain't many of us left."